[it's time to] Defeat [your] Debt

HAS ANY BODY CHECKED THE FOUNDATION?

Debt Prevention & Elimination for Families

By Gary & Drenda Keesee of Faith-Full Family Finances

Dedicated to those who feel hopeless as we once did … there is hope!

Additional copies may be obtained from Faith-Full Family Finances, Inc.
1-888-397-DEBT
www.faith-fullfamilyfinances.com

Published by

FreeIndeed

Publishing

6040 Sharp Rd. Mt. Vernon, OH 43050
(740) 397-3328

Printed in the U.S.A.

Table of Contents

Introduction: Our Story 1

1. Debt: Satan's Deception 3

2. The Price We Pay 9

3. Debt: A Way of Life 17

4. The Curse of Poverty 23

5. What Does the Bible Say? 31

6. Kingdom Laws: Sowing & Reaping 37

7. No One Can Serve Two Masters 51

8. Faith and Patience: God's Promotion System ... 53

9. Which Kingdom? 59

10. The Economy of God 67

11. Getting Started 73

12. The Steps to Freedom 75

Appendix: The Plan

Our Story

A few years ago, we were just another ordinary family in debt. We did not have extra money in the bank–we had credit cards instead. We had no cash reserve and no written budget. We lived paycheck to paycheck. When we were short of cash, we used credit to make up the difference, thinking the next week would be better. Before long, we found that our reliance on debt was slowly putting us in chains. We were dying financially, and let me say that you cannot die financially without dying emotionally. We were in such bondage that I lived in constant despair. It seemed that all hope was gone. If you have ever been there, you understand what I am saying. If you have never been in that place of hopelessness, then I pray you never will.

Like most people, we did not set out to destroy our lives through debt. We had real needs that we were trying to meet to the best of our abilities. We did not live extravagantly, but we had to obtain the necessities of life somehow. Since everyone else used debt, we did not feel guilty about borrowing for such necessities. Besides, we were sure that we could pay the debt back when times got better. We thought of it as a normal way of life.

I can remember many times going to the bank to beg for a short-term note to carry us through until the next paycheck. There were days that we bought our food with gas station credit cards. You know–we bought those cellophane sandwiches that leave much to be desired! Many times, we could not pay the bills, so we used debt to pay debt. I can clearly remember the smothering feeling of failure and despair that told me I was an inadequate breadwinner for my wife and three children. *Why am I such a loser?* I thought. I was a Christian who loved God, and I tithed and gave offerings to the church. I also served in the church. What was I doing wrong?

As I cried out to the Lord for help, He began to speak to me concerning my situation. First, He made it very clear that He had not caused my financial difficulty. **I had fallen into this trap by myself because I had leaned to the wrong system of trust.** He also let me know that He would deliver me from my debt if I would humble myself before Him and follow His instructions.

Obeying His instructions was not always easy, but it brought peace. It required many changes, such as selling my house and relocating a thousand miles to a new city. It involved starting a business from scratch that I knew little about. Most of all, it involved learning God's Word and learning how to trust Him for my needs instead of trusting in debt. He taught me many valuable lessons that changed my life. This book was written to help you understand those lessons and principles that have helped me lay aside every weight and better fulfill my destiny in Christ. **I wouldn't give anything for the journey because it was in these times that I learned to hear and follow His voice.**

Chapter 1   Debt: Satan's Deception

With every plan and principle of God, there is a counterfeit and a temptation to walk in fear and our own strength. I believe the greatest deception used by Satan to destroy people's lives today is the widespread use of debt. You may ask how I can make such a statement. Let me show you a verse in the book of Lamentations.

Lamentations 3:17
I have been deprived of peace; I have forgotten what prosperity is.

Some say that money is not important and that everything is spiritual. Well, I would say to them that having more to give to others *is* spiritual. It is hard to have peace when a need is staring you down. When you see that your child needs orthodontic treatment or essentials of life and you cannot provide those things, it grieves you. This life requires money.

So many people are under great stress because of debt. Debt steals their peace by demanding more and more of their labor (life). Debt has become a way of life in America. I am sorry to say that the church has also adopted this lifestyle. The effect on the family is mind-boggling, but one of the most prevalent aspects of this epidemic is the hopelessness that abounds in every American home. Families have lost their dreams and zeal for life. All the money coming in is now used to pay bills, and there is nothing left over with which to save or dream about the future. For many, the joy in life is gone.

I can still remember as a child going behind our home, where a housing project was under way, and collecting pop bottles to sell. I would gather them until I had enough money saved to pay for the mail-order rocket I planned to buy. While picking up the bottles, I greatly anticipated the enjoyment ahead. I worked with excitement because of my vision. God intended for us to enjoy our occupation and work, and in so doing, we find our greatest fulfillment. However, in America it is a well documented fact that most people are employed in jobs they dislike because they are boxed in by debt payments and responsibilities. Many people would rather be doing something else with their lives. Instead, life has become one big rat race to pay the creditor.

Proverbs 17:1

Better is a dry crust of bread with peace and quiet than a house full of feasting with strife.

The Bible speaks of contentment along with godliness as something of great gain. In contentment, fulfillment and peace can be found. However, in America we are not content; we want many things. Lust is never fulfilled. There is no house or car that can fulfill the demand of the lust for things. There is always going to be a faster car, a bigger house, and people who seem to have it better than us. Jesus said in Mark 4 that the deceitfulness of riches chokes out the Word of God. Most Christians I have met think they will be happy if they can just get some thing. Truly, things can be a blessing, but true happiness comes from who we are in Christ and not what we possess. I have learned to be content with what I have, when I have it. The apostle Paul said, "I have learned in whatsoever state I am in therewith to be content." This is not to be confused with the term "satisfied." God has created us to always be advancing forward, and "being content" does not mean we should stagnate and be satisfied with a lack of advancement. We simply need to be content as we progress forward in God. Jesus should be our contentment because He is our life.

The quest for material things and success in America has become the idol of the land. Families have been trained to sacrifice their home life and their relationships to have the things they want or the things they think they need. I remember a Daffy Duck cartoon where the devil promises to give Daffy fame and fortune if he will sell his soul. This cartoon portrays the same mentality as that of relying on debt. Even if we do not have the money, if we sell our future to the lender, he will get us what we want today. This kind of lifestyle brings with it inevitable bondage to the debtor. A recent article stated that the baby boom generation is not saving money at all. Only two out of ten families manage to save $1,000 over a year's period of time. We live in a consumer generation with only one main objective: to have the most and enjoy the most. Debt seems to offer a shortcut to obtain this way of life.

America is endorsing debt as a lifestyle with no regard for the end result. The country itself has relied on debt to fund the government for over 25 years, building its own debt to a whopping 7 trillion dollars. To illustrate the enormity of this number, let's look at the following example. If you were to count 1, 2, 3…, just how long do you think it would take to count to 1 trillion? The answer is 31,685 years. As you can see, this debt will never be retired! Future generations will be saddled with paying it back in the form of escalating taxes or possibly by forfeiting the freedoms we have in America today.

The American family is in a situation proportionate to the government's dire financial state. We use 30-year mortgages to finance our homes and 7-year car loans to buy our cars. Visa pays for our clothing, and finance companies supply our carpeting and furniture. Basically, debt can instantly purchase anything we want. Most families never get out of debt. They simply trade-up for nicer things throughout their lifetime, finance the upgrade, and then retire in debt.

Because of the quick availability of financing, the national work ethic and the worth of a dollar have been devalued in this country. If the only requirement for making a purchase is signing a piece of paper, we will respect that item proportionately with the amount of labor it takes to replace it. What makes a painting valuable? The hand-skilled labor and the rarity of the painting are what give it worth. Because debt makes things so accessible and replaceable, we do not need much labor to obtain something new. Our view of life and the value of work have been affected by the ease with which we spend.

Debt forces the price of things to keep escalating. If purchases were only made with cash, people would think twice about spending money. For a car, we can rationalize a payment of $199.00 per month much easier than a price tag of $30,000. How expensive could the market price of a home soar if every buyer had to have cash instead of financing? The utilization of debt drives prices higher. More people think they can "afford" to pay the greater cost for purchases because they view the price in monthly installments. This slow destruction of the work ethic and the escalation of prices are eroding the foundation on which our great country was founded.

During The Great Depression, people would search for employment for weeks. Today, instead of looking for work, some people may look for the nearest government office to give them a handout. Somehow, we have trained our citizens that it is the government's responsibility to provide for us without requiring us to put forth some effort. This increasing dependence on the government takes more and more tax dollars from the family. Our government also has a progressive tax structure, which penalizes those who have become successful through hard work. This requires a greater tax percentage of that wealth to be given to those who have not paid the same price. Do not misunderstand me, I am in favor of helping those in need, but I believe in helping people just long enough to enable them to become self-sufficient.

It is not helpful to eliminate all the struggles in people's lives. It is the struggle and the risks taken that change and transform a life. Self-esteem is gained not by a welfare check but by becoming someone, by feeling good about yourself and by appreciating the things you have learned about life. By having a system where everyone has a chance to make it–knowing that hard work will pay off–we guarantee to those following our generation that they will have the same freedoms we enjoy. Debt gives people all the things that success offers without requiring them to pay the price to succeed. By allowing debt to eliminate the hunger that drives people to succeed, we have affected their future and stunted their growth.

In addition to putting families in bondage to the lender, debt's greatest danger to our future may be the social change it has brought to the values in this country. My grandmother would always say, "A penny saved is a penny earned." Today, people do not worry about saving pennies. In Grandma's generation, I can remember the jar in the window where the spare change was saved for buying milk and bread. They had no credit cards; they understood the worth of a dollar and the value of hard work. Credit cards have forever changed the way we view savings and work. The new attitude says that you do not need cash to buy goods. This mindset opens the door to financial bondage.

Amazingly, credit card debt is somewhat a young invention. The first credit card, "The Diner's Club," started in 1949. Now just 50 years later, credit cards are a dime a dozen, and most families have multiple cards that are charged to the limit. Frequently I hear people say, "If it wasn't for credit, we wouldn't have anything." I always tell people that they still don't have anything. Stop making the payment, and the legal, rightful owner will come and take the property away.

Debt paints a false image of success. With debt, anyone can exhibit prosperity for a season, but eventually, the truth will come out. When I was in the financial planning business, I can still remember pulling up to a large home with a Jaguar in the driveway. As I pulled in, I thought, *Why have they invited me here? It seems they're doing fine.* As I spoke to the couple about their finances, the wife broke into tears and said they could not keep going as they had been. Monthly payments to creditors along with back taxes and stress had taken a toll on their home life. It was at that moment I decided to never be intimidated again by what someone seems to own or the title of their occupation. I am sure that you have heard about many professional athletes who made millions but ended up broke. Their character was not mature enough to handle wealth with wisdom, so they lost everything.

It does not always matter what you make, but rather what you spend that determines the freedom you enjoy. I have met with thousands of families, and the sad truth is it does not matter what their income or profession is, most are severely in debt and are closer to financial trouble than they realize. The good life in America is portrayed as a life full of things and leisure, but I don't think anyone truly understands the price we pay for the attitudes we nurture. I have found that freedom is of greater value than things, if by acquiring those things, we have put ourselves in slavery.

Chapter 2

The Price We Pay

Probably the most devastating impact of financial stress can be seen in the breakdown of marriages and family relationships. If you are married, then you already know the effect that money (or the lack of it) has on your marriage. In 1990, 55 percent of all marriages in Columbus, Ohio ended in divorce, and 80 percent of those divorces attributed the cause to financial stress. You cannot live on this earth without acknowledging the role of money and its effect on your life. Jesus recognized the needs that people had, and He spent a large portion of His ministry teaching on money, servitude and showed how we are to meet those needs today. We will give attention to His answers for life's needs in a later chapter.

Most people derive their self-esteem from the things they have and their position on the corporate ladder. As a follower of Christ, our goals and ambitions must be established in correct priority if we are to have good success. I have been in many homes where the budget is stretched extremely tight, but a brand new car with a $500 payment is sitting in the driveway. Why would a family do such a thing? The reason: status and maligned priorities.

I remember the time I drove up to a church to visit the pastor. There were only three cars in the parking lot, and one of them was a brand-new, 5-speed, red convertible with leather interior and loaded. I went into the church and I saw Jane, a woman whom I knew because two weeks earlier she had asked me for $100 so she could give to a special project at church. She was a single parent, and money was tight. I asked Jane if she knew whose car was in the lot. With a sheepish look, she said that it was hers. I could not believe it! The temporary tags on the car had a date of only two days earlier. This was the same woman that had asked me for money only two weeks before. I asked Jane how much a car like that costs, and she said $28,000. Her next statement shocked me. She said, "Don't worry, I didn't buy the car. I just leased it." I asked her what the payment was, and she said $500 a month. My mouth must have fallen open because then she said, "God told me to buy that car." I walked away shaking my head, for I knew that God would not be so unwise in counsel. Why would she do such a thing? She wanted to be someone, and that car made her feel special. I knew she would not be feeling too good about herself in future when she would have to deal with making a $500 payment from her budget.

We all want to appear successful. God has placed the desire to succeed within each of us because God is a God of victory and success. Children do not play bankruptcy court; they pretend they are heroes, winners and presidents. Children dream of victory as they grow up. It is only when life beats us around for awhile and we fail to apply faith in the Word of God that we begin to lose our hope, our zeal, and our hunger for life. Instead of *living* life, we just try to *survive* life. Our self-esteem seems to be tied to how well we are doing, and we will do anything to appear successful to other people. When we try to keep up with the Jones', we open ourselves up to a snare of Satan. We must come to the realization that the possessions we own do not make us a winner or success. Proverbs says, "The fear of man causes a snare." If we live our lives to please men instead of God, we will always come out discouraged, disappointed, and disillusioned. We are to pattern our lives after the Word of God and not after the world's definition of success. We are not going to stand before our neighbors and give an account, but we will stand before the Lord God Almighty. Many times, people who are struggling financially find that their self-esteem begins to erode. I believe this is one of the key reasons for the prevalent "mid-life crisis." Money makes a horrible master. Jesus said in **Matthew 6:24:**

No one can serve two masters. Either he will hate the one and love the other, or he will be devoted to the one and despise the other. You cannot serve both God and Money.

Because people think that having money will solve all of their problems, they look to it as their source. They serve it, or as Jesus said, they run after it. That means they make decisions and choose careers based on money instead of stopping to consider where God may be directing them. God wants to be our source. Jesus said if we serve God, He will give us the *same things* that the pagans serve money to obtain. The problem with serving money is that in itself, it does not bring contentment. It is only when we are in the right place, the place that God has created for us, that we find contentment. Since so many people base their decisions on security or money instead of what God has for them, they are discontent, and this discontentment shows up in what the world calls a mid-life crisis. A mid-life crisis is nothing more than an identity crisis. People struggle with the purpose of their lives. They know it is worth more than punching a time clock just to make money, but what? Without God they will never truly find contentment and purpose.

The results of discontentment, such as stress, hopelessness, and rebellion against God, are a few of the problems that surface from serving money. We should fight to keep this kind of destruction out of our homes at all costs.

Debt–obtaining money through slavery–attacks the fabric of the home. For many, instead of the home being a refuge from life's pressures, it is a stress-filled environment–a war zone. We can see a symptom of this financial stress in the fact that so many husbands turn over the responsibility of juggling the strained budget to their wives. The response to fear and the pressure of finances find an escape route in the wife, whom God made to have a desire to help her husband. Although this may seem harmless, seeds of destruction are being planted in the home.

I estimate that in approximately 80 percent of the families I have counseled, the wife paid the bills. I do not mean she wrote the checks and mailed them–I mean she handled the bills. She felt the pressure to make sure the bills were paid, and she was the one left with the responsibility to work out any details or problems with creditors. Although women are generally better with details, this gifting was meant to function under the protection and leadership of the husband. A woman was not made to handle the pressure and stress of this role by herself. Being emotionally based, the stress will eventually surface at a time when the husband least expects it. It will most likely be over a very small matter, and an explosion will result. The husband will shake his head and won't be able to understand why she blew up over such a small issue. The fact is the pressure was building, and she could not take any more. Resentment toward his lack of protection and leadership simply found a vent. This fit of rage is a symptom of a greater problem in the marriage.

Since man's greatest needs in marriage revolve around the wife (his need to be respected and his sexual drive), these needs will suffer. Consequently, he will become unfulfilled in life. A man who does not feel secure at home will find it hard to be a conqueror in a world of insecurity. Most of the time, the husband does not even realize he is the cause of such unrest at home, so he blames it on his wife's emotional instability and lack of submission. I believe that this role reversal is one of the key factors in the increasing depression among women. The era of the super-mom is taking its toll! Yes, it is easier to delegate the financial stress, and in many cases, she welcomes it; but when the husband does this, the home steps out of divine order and is open to deception and attack from Satan.

Many times I've observed a wife rebel against her husband's leadership because he put her under the financial gun by delegating to her his God-ordained role as the provider. I am shocked at how many Christian men insist that their wives work outside the home. Thus, by increasing the number of mothers in the workforce, the fabric of family life is torn. Currently, 70 percent of all mothers with children over six years old work outside the home in America. For 75 percent of all children, other caregivers spend more time with them than their own mothers. The impact of mom's absence can be seen in youth on every level of society. An interesting fact I spotted in *USA Today* stated that currently 86 percent of all new homebuyers are families where both spouses work outside the home. Again, the society we live in pushes people toward its values unless they lean to the Word of God and ask the Lord for wisdom.

One of the most damaging effects of debt is its attack on our faith. People ask, "Why isn't God meeting my needs?" I will discuss this issue in more detail later on, but many Christians have abandoned the faith just as Paul warned.

1 Timothy 6:9,10
People who want to get rich fall into temptation and a trap and into many foolish and harmful desires that plunge men into ruin and destruction. For the love of money is a root of all kinds of evil. Some people eager for money have wandered from the faith and pierced themselves with many griefs.

Once we take our eyes off Jesus and begin to seek after the things of this life as our priorities, then the Word says that we open ourselves up to ruin and destruction. Once we have started down that road, debt offers the fulfillment of our desires. Debt is a hard taskmaster, and financial bondage becomes one of the many griefs of wandering from the faith. However, Jesus never said you were to go through life without the things that pertain to life and godliness. You do not have to bow to debt to have all that you need.

Let me share with you the state in which I have found the average family in America. After spending 23 years helping families, I have found that the average American lives month-to-month with about $50 to $100 extra in their budget with which to enjoy life. They have no cash reserve to protect themselves against possible emergencies. **Ecclesiastes 7:12** says that money is a defense. With no cash reserve, they are open to an attack and will suffer loss. Building an adequate cash reserve is one of the first steps I advise a family to take. This is not as difficult as one may think, and we will discuss how to fund this reserve in a later chapter.

I have found that 99 percent of the families I give assistance to do not have a written budget. The credit card has made it easy to disregard this budgeting tool of the past. If the budget is tight, the credit card makes up the difference for most families. I found an interesting study in *Reader's Digest* (August 1999) stating that 95 percent of a family's disposable income is already allocated to debt payments. One of the first things I ask a family to do is show me a budget, since most families state they have a few hundred extra dollars each month. After I have them produce a budget for me, I find that they are actually hundreds of dollars short. How can this be? How could they not know? The answer is that there is no longer an absolute bottom line to gauge whether a family can afford expenditure or not. If they want it, there is a way they can get it through credit, and thus, the budget for most is a fuzzy gray area. As it has been said, "As long as I have checks or credit cards, I have money."

This has led to the explosive growth of the credit card industry. According to *The Columbus Dispatch*, there are ten credit cards for every family in America, four of which are bankcards, with an average balance of over $2,000. For many families, credit cards are even used to pay debt payments on time. When a family comes to this point, they are already in serious trouble.

With both spouses working and their budget dependent on the dual-income, they have no security. If one of them loses their job, the house payment is in jeopardy. I believe the average family is about two to four months away from going into foreclosure. Living under this constant financial fear over time has a negative effect on people. I believe this could be a key door that the spirit of fear uses to invade a person's life. Fear just needs an avenue to make its attack.

For years, I lived under great fear over money, and I had extreme anxiety in my life. My wife would come home from the store in fear of my reaction to the amount of money she had spent for groceries or other needs. This was bondage for her and for me. Thank God, Christ has set me free from the spirit of fear.

I talked with a dentist about this epidemic of fear in our land. He said that 6 out of 10 of his dental clients were on drugs that dealt with fear or depression. Doctors do not have answers for this fear and pressure that people live under. Unless a person deals with the underlying root of the problem–which is spiritual–he will never truly recover. The drugs may mask some of the symptoms, but the problem will still be there.

Luke 12:32

Do not fear little flock for it is your Father's good pleasure to give you the kingdom.

You have probably heard stories of older people who lived through the Great Depression and who later continued to live as paupers despite the fact that they had thousands of dollars in every bank in town. The spirit of fear gained an entrance into their lives during a time of financial worry and warped their thinking in such a way that they feared spending any money. Since they had placed their trust in money, they had become enslaved to the fear of losing it. My wife and I knew an older woman who had hundreds of thousands of dollars in the bank but lived like she was very poor. She existed in constant fear. She had six to seven dead bolt locks on her doors, and even the doors in the house that went from room to room had three to four dead bolts on them. She would lock herself in the innermost room with all the locks secured to try to find peace. I don't believe she ever found it.

When I was growing up, one of the best investments was a home. Part of the American dream is to own a home, yet only two percent of the homes in America are paid off. Another disturbing fact recorded in *Newsweek* stated that the average 62-year-old has only $2,300 in the bank and still owes 22 years on his first mortgage. Although the homes and cars in America look great, underneath the surface, the American family is not making it!

I remember thinking if I could just make $50,000 a year, all my financial problems would be over. Well, I eventually did make $50,000 a year, and guess what? My financial problems were worse! *Time Magazine* stated, "The average family making $50,000 a year has only $1,200 saved in the bank." It doesn't matter how much you make–it matters how much you spend!

Due to our consuming lifestyles and our reliance on debt, 87 percent of the people retiring in this country retire under the poverty level, and 40 percent of them are forced to live on less than $700 a month. If you think this fact is disturbing, realize it could happen to you unless you have a plan to do otherwise.

Proverbs 10:22

The blessing of the Lord maketh rich and he adds no sorrow to it.

It's not too late to give your life a fresh start, regardless of your age, and make a determination to prosper God's way. I have found that the only way to succeed without compromising in any arena of life is to submit to His plan for my success. Some people have money but have little else and neglect their families to pursue wealth. Others seem to have good families but lack financial success. God's ways bring peace and prosperity without sorrow attached. Ideally, if we do it God's way from the beginning, we can avoid taking years to recover from errors and heartache. In our tenth year of marriage, we were so happy to finally get back to the place where we started–owing no one. It is so sad that we had to learn the hard way. We would have been so much further ahead if we would have been taught these principles at an early age.

I have observed many families. After marriage, there seems to be a predictable path that most couples take. I call it "the five-year path to slavery." A young couple is excited about life, and they have many dreams and aspirations. Very quickly, they want all the things they think will bring them happiness. Unknowingly, many of these early decisions will eventually take them into divorce court. After about five years of marriage, this same couple has discovered that life is more difficult than they thought possible. They now have two car payments and a house payment. In addition, they owe Visa, a finance company, relatives and more bills. Because their lifestyle is based on both of their incomes, when children enter the picture, mom must go back to work after maternity leave. Her heart is torn between being a mother and an employee. The stress has an impact on her husband as well. He hasn't moved up into the higher paying positions as quickly as he desires, so he has to take a part-time job to make ends meet. The stress gets tougher and tougher until finally the partners begin to blame each other for the stress. The tightening pressure means the end of their marriage may be near. Unfortunately, this happens every day!

God did not intend for our lives to be full of strife and stress. How has the family allowed such a deceptive lifestyle to overtake them? This deception comes through a barrage of media messages that define success for our culture. You will become what you mediate upon. If you renew your mind to the Word of God, you will reflect His life to the world. Unfortunately, if you spend your efforts and time in the world, you will reflect the world's views in your life.

Romans 12:2
Do not conform any longer to the pattern of this world, but be transformed by the renewing of your mind.

Chapter **3**

DEBT: A Way of Life

Again, let me repeat a simple fact: America has made credit a way of life. Advertisers use all kinds of gimmicks to sell their products, utilizing debt as a form of payment. Tactics such as "90-days-same-as-cash," "no payments until the year 2010," rebates and "easy terms" are just a few of the ploys used. Most advertisers sell their products with a payment plan rather than a lump sum price. Watch any television advertisement selling cars, and you will find that the car is always sold with a monthly payment, not the total price. The same holds true in a department store that handles large ticket items such as stoves and freezers. Again, we see the monthly payment marketing technique used effectively. Since most people do not have any money on hand, a payment plan is the only way the retailers can tempt most folks to buy.

Since most people do not have enough money to buy the things they want or need, the availability of credit has become extremely important. As a result, credit has become a status symbol in this country. You will find many colored credit cards on the market, each with its unique appeal to human self-esteem. The inference is that a gold platinum card makes you "somebody," whereas a drab green card means that you are just one among the masses. Credit is the ticket to our dreams. However, most lenders don't show us that the dream purchased with credit slowly but surely becomes a choking nightmare.

Visa and Mastercard have successfully brainwashed millions into believing that "you deserve it" and "you should not leave home without it." Ultimately, what they want is for you to use their card and not pay it off in the interest-free 30-day period of time. They understand human nature only too well.

The 90-days-same-as-cash appeal sounds harmless. I ask people all the time, "What makes you think you will be able to pay for something in 90 days when you can't pay for it now? Is there going to be some windfall of money in the next few weeks?"

I had a friend who went to a local electronics store to look at computers. He was not planning to buy anything–he was just looking. He walked out with a computer and a 90-days-same-as-cash agreement. Of course in 90 days, he then found himself with a payment at 28 percent interest! He would never have bought the computer if he would have had to sign a 28 percent agreement at the time of purchase. Human nature is predictable and easily exploited by the retailers.

Let me make one point clear–someone wants you in debt! As an example, Sears Department Stores charge 21 percent on their credit cards. There is no bank that will pay a depositor 21 percent on their deposits. Sears has found a way to invest their money at 21 percent in a market that should normally be paying 8 percent interest. By the way, Sears makes more money on the interest from the credit cards than the mark-up on the retail item they sell to you. You may have also noticed that if you make a payment higher than the required amount due on the monthly credit card statement, the next monthly bill has a minimum payment of zero due. Sears is not ignorant; they don't want you to pay the card off. If you have a balance of $4,500 on the card, it will take 33 years to pay it off if you make the minimum payment. Of course, this is assuming that you do not use the card again, which is normally a false assumption. If you are like the average consumer, Sears will have money coming in from you at 21 percent interest for most of your life.

To lenders, credit is a highly lucrative business! There are highly paid professionals with one job and that is to devise methods of extracting your money. Basically, the motivation behind advertising is to first cause you to want the item and then provide a way for you to obtain it.

The emergence of credit has become such an important issue in our society that the credit report has become highly esteemed as well. Protecting the credit report and correcting any bad credit has become big business. I tell many people who are in bad financial shape that the best thing they ever did for themselves was destroy their credit. It managed to stop their self-destructive habits and end their reliance upon debt as their source of provision.

Again, families do not have disposable money. The federal government relies on this fact when it sets economic policy. When President Bush wanted to stimulate the economy in 1993, he reduced the withholding formula for payroll checks. This put more cash into the hands of the American worker, although it did not reduce taxes. President Bush knew that any money added to the paycheck of Americans would be spent, thus propelling the economy. The Federal Reserve stimulates the economy by lowering interest rates. If the entire truth were known concerning just how deeply this lifestyle of debt has affected our culture, we would be shocked.

America is an idolatrous nation. The good life in America is portrayed as a life of things and leisure. Actually, it is a life of selfishness and consumption. Of course, debt funds the American way of life. The attitudes in America are becoming increasingly self-indulgent. America's standards and viewpoints can be read from the bumper stickers that people put on their cars. I have listed a few below that exemplify our country's attitudes:

"I'm keeping up with the Jones'."

This is a typical bumper sticker that portrays a way of life in America. We all want to appear successful to our peers, so it becomes important what size our house is or what type of car we drive. My warning to you is, "I have been to the Jones' house and have seen their financial books. If something went wrong at work, they would be only a few months away from bankruptcy." I tell people, "I have been there, and you do not want to keep up with the Jones'. They live a very precarious lifestyle, certainly one that does not promote peace of mind."

"I owe, I owe, so off to work I go."

…A very true statement. America has sold itself into slavery, and we have lost our future options. A slave does not have any options but rather works for his master. A slave cannot decide when and where he is going to work. He must report to work when the master commands. In light of the debt epidemic, this bumper sticker is accurate. I still don't understand why anyone would want to admit this by placing it on the back of his or her car for the world to see.

Again, this is a very ungodly and selfish declaration, considering the scripture below.

Proverbs 13:22
A good man leaves an inheritance for his children's children, but a sinner's wealth is stored up for the righteous.

God wants us to work hard and invest wisely. The fact that we have an inheritance to pass on is a testimony to God. It implies that God has prospered us, and we have taken the counsel of the Lord during our lives. Since most people retire broke, it is evident that they did not take wise counsel of the Lord. Using debt as a way of life is a defiance of God's wisdom since His Word does not endorse that lifestyle. Living in debt is the main reason people retire broke in this country. It is sad, but we have given our labor away to others at the expense of our future.

I saw an interesting bumper sticker one day while pulling into a McDonald's restaurant. On one corner of the bumper it read, "Save the Whales," and "Pro-Choice." On the other corner, the stickers said, "Our Mother the Earth" and "Animals have feelings, too." The irony was that this person was at the drive-thru window picking up a cheeseburger–a dead cow (with feelings too, I might add). America has some warped ideas about life. The bottom line is that America needs Jesus. We Christians need to be the ones to tell them the truth. We are called to be salt and light to a mixed-up, perverse generation.

Proverbs 14:12
There is a way that seems right to a man but in the end is destruction.

Debt is a way that may seem right, but in the end you will find destruction. One of the most incredible stories I have ever heard concerning destruction from debt was told to me a couple of years ago. After finishing a radio talk show one day, I received a call from a man who asked me to come by his home for a talk. He told me that when he was a young man, he received a credit card in the mail. He did not request the card; it simply arrived in his mailbox with a credit limit of

$20,000. He did not have a job at the time, so he decided to take off on a world tour. After traveling around awhile, he ended up in England where he met a girl and fell in love. He lied to her and told her that he was a very successful businessman from America. They got married and later had a child. He never did get a job. He would leave in the morning and come back in the evening pretending he was going to work. He continued this delusion by living on cash advances from the credit cards that kept coming in the mail. This went on for four years! The man told me he was afraid that if he ever told his wife the truth, she would leave him.

Eventually he ran out of credit cards. In desperation, he forged his brother's name to four credit cards. A few months later, he received a call from the local authorities wanting him for credit card fraud. He had incurred $270,000 in credit card debt! He went to prison for 6 months, during which time he came to know the Lord Jesus Christ. His wife also came to know the Lord during this time period. They are happily married today, but he told me to warn people about debt. He said he never intended to destroy his life with a Visa Card. Most people never intend to destroy their lives. Destruction is a result of sin and disregard for God's counsel. God gave us His Word so that we could see the direction to take and avoid disaster.

I had another friend who went to a local department store to purchase some shoes. The store turned down his credit card. He insisted that there must be some mistake. After checking with Visa, they assured him that the card was over the limit. He went home and promptly asked his wife about the payment, since she handled all of the bills. She began to cry and brought a shoebox from the bedroom with 43 credit cards in it. She had rung up $43,000 on these cards without him even knowing it! They had to declare bankruptcy, and their marriage ended in divorce. This is a surprisingly typical example of destruction in which debt was a key player.

I had another acquaintance that accumulated $125,000 in credit card debt without her husband's knowledge. They also ended their marriage in divorce court.

The Bible is a relevant book for today, and the wages of sin is still death without the Lord Jesus Christ. Satan knows human nature very well. He knows how to tempt you and entice you towards your fleshly desires. Jesus came to set us free from the law of sin and death, and He gave us His Word and a living example with which to renew our minds.

Luke 4:18.21

The spirit of the Lord is upon me, because he has anointed me to <u>preach the gospel (good news) to the poor,</u> he has sent me to heal the brokenhearted, to preach deliverance to the captives, and recovering of sight to the blind, to set at liberty them that are bruised, to preach the acceptable year of the Lord.

Jesus preached freedom to the captive and good news to the poor man. What would be good news to the poor man? *You do not have to borrow your way through life and be a second-class citizen any longer!* The acceptable year of the Lord was the year of Jubilee when all the slaves were set free. Jesus offers us a new beginning and a covenant that promises the blessing of God to those who will believe and obey Him.

To get a better understanding of our covenant, let's go back to the beginning, to the book of Genesis.

Chapter **4** The Curse of Poverty

Some churches teach that being wealthy is wrong. They assume anyone who has become wealthy must have taken advantage of someone else to do so. Everyone knows that rich people are greedy and prideful. This is the view many people have of those who have money. Some religious circles feel that it is godly to be poor. They point to the story of the rich young ruler and to the statement that Jesus made concerning how hard it was for someone who was rich to enter the kingdom of heaven. But was the sin of the rich young ruler his wealth? Or was it that his wealth had him? His trust was in his riches. Anyone who has been in financial stress knows that it is a curse. It is not a blessing. Most people have lived hand-to-mouth for so long, they know no other way. Yes, we have developed some degree of ability in making it by. We have learned how to "rob Peter to pay Paul," but this is not God's best. God told the Israelites that they would be lenders and not borrowers. Israel's wealth would testify to the heathen nations of God's faithfulness. Was man destined to just "get by" day by day? NO! It started in the Garden of Eden.

Genesis 3:17

To Adam he said, "Because you listened to your wife and ate from the tree about which I commanded you, 'You must not eat of it.' Cursed is the ground because of you; <u>through painful toil you will eat of it all the days of your life. It will produce thorns and thistles for you,</u> and you will eat the plants of the field. By the sweat of your brow you will eat your food until you return to the ground, for dust you are and to dust you will return."

Here we see the curse pronounced by God over Adam after he sinned. Before the fall, mankind took no real concern over the things he needed in life. Father God gave everything to Adam in the garden. Notice the curse says that Adam must continually toil to eat. There was no plentiful harvest and no time to take a break from toiling. By the sweat of his brow, Adam would eat. The Bible says it would be this way for <u>all of the days of his life.</u>

We must acknowledge that this curse came on the earth because of what Adam had done; it was not God's idea. This curse was a curse of poverty, just getting by, no hope of ever really prospering in life. Hopelessness sums up the feelings Adam had when God spoke these words to him. Maybe it is how you feel today.

It amazes me that many Christians still think money is evil, and to be righteous you must have your needs met–no more. My friend, this is the curse Adam received; don't settle for this kind of lifestyle. To understand how man has a way out of this curse, we must remember that God gave the dominion of the earth to Adam. Adam had legal right to live here. We can see this in the following scripture:

Hebrews 2:6
But there is a place where someone has testified: "What is man that you are mindful of him, the son of man that you care for him? You made him a little lower than the angels [Elohim]; you crowned him with glory and honor and put EVERYTHING UNDER HIS FEET."

It is important you understand that man had complete dominion over the earth. Everything was under his feet. God said to Adam, "Because of you" the curse came on the earth. God did not bring it on the earth–mankind did. Many people, not understanding this dominion issue, have blamed God for not stopping wars or other trouble on the earth. Of course God has the power to stop wars, but He can't violate the authority to rule that he gave to Adam (man). God does not go back on his Word. He gave men dominion on the earth, and if men start wars then men must stop them.

God must use inspired and anointed people on the earth to do His will, just as Satan must use demon-inspired people to do his will. God is bound by His Word. God could not stop Adam from sinning in the first place–it was Adam's choice. The only way God can legally influence man is by invitation. I know that may sound strange to you, but if it were not true, the Bible would not say in **Acts 2:21**–
And everyone who calls on the name of the Lord will be saved.

We know it is God's will that all men be saved. Why must God wait until a man calls on His name to be saved?

2 Timothy 2:4

God our Savior, who wants all men to be saved and to come to the knowledge of the truth.

Why doesn't God just appear in the sky and tell men the plan of salvation or better yet make them repent? The answer: He can't! He has given men dominion over the earth. If you leased a home, the landlord could not drop in whenever he wanted. You have legal rights. This covenant we have is a legal document–an agreement between God and man, and God will honor His covenant legally. Let me give you another example.

You must realize that Satan hates a believer on the earth. A believer in heaven poses no threat to him, but a believer on the earth has authority to destroy His kingdom. Why doesn't Satan just kill every believer or kill every man or woman before they have a chance to hear the gospel? He can't! Let's look at **1 Peter 5:8:**

*Be self-controlled and alert. Your enemy the devil prowls around like a roaring lion **LOOKING** for someone to devour.*

Satan can't kill you. If he had that authority, he would have already done it. He looks for those he can devour. What is he looking for? He is looking for people who give him legal right to devour. Sin is an example of what he needs to gain legal access to someone's life. Sin opens the door for Satan to devour.

James 5:15

And the prayer offered in faith will make the sick person well; the Lord will raise him up. If he has sinned, he will be forgiven. Therefore confess your sins to each other and pray for each other so that you may be healed.

Here we see that sin may have been the reason that the person became sick. We also see that by confessing sin, God is able to heal us. Invert that and we see that by hiding sin, Satan has a right to devour us. Most people think that God can do anything He wants, when He wants. Come on now, He is God, isn't He? Yes, He is God, and He has revealed to us what is legally ours and how to obtain justice through His Word.

Now that we understand the legal access to the earth is through mankind, we see why God had to find a man that would make a covenant with him. This would give God a legal doorway through which He could bring His salvation to man. That man was Abram, later to become Abraham. Here was a man who believed what God said above what he could see with his own senses. This belief was credited to Abram as righteousness or right standing with God. Because Abram believed God over earth's circumstances, God had a legal right to make a covenant with him. Satan could not stop God from making a covenant (a legal agreement) with Abram. God had used this same law of dominion to obtain entrance into the earth through Adam. You see, Satan found a man who would believe him when he cast doubt on the Word of God–Adam. Now God had a man who would open that door back up to the earth–a man who would believe Him at all costs–Abram.

As a matter of legal access into the earth, Jesus "had to" enter the earth in a flesh body. If you follow Jesus in His ministry, He always referred to Himself as the son of man, not the Son of God. Only the demons, which knew Him in His true power and authority, called Him the Son of God. Every time this happened, Jesus told them to be quiet. Jesus the Son of God had to take on flesh as a man to pay the price in this earth realm for sin. Because God's own decree sentenced man to death if he sinned, God could not restore man to his place of authority and son-ship that Adam had lost unless an innocent man was willing to die in his place and pay the price for Adam's sin. No man born of man was able to do this because of the spiritual death that was in mankind.

Jesus was born of a virgin and had a different father than Adam. His human spirit was alive to God from conception. Look at what the Bible says about the birth of Jesus.

Matthew 4:1

The people living in darkness have seen a great light; on those living in the land of the shadow of death a light has dawned.

This was the first light–"the life of God"–seen in a man since Adam. Although men had been anointed with the Holy Spirit in the Old Testament, none had the life of God in them in this way. This is why Jesus is called the second Adam. By making a covenant with Abram, God had a legal door to bring Jesus into the earth to save mankind. Let's take a look at the covenant God made with Abram.

Genesis 12:2

I will make you into a great nation and I will bless you; I will make your name great, and you will BE A BLESSING. I will bless those who bless you, and whoever curses you I will curse; and all peoples on earth will be blessed through you.

Notice that it says that all peoples on the earth would be blessed "through" Abraham. The word "through" refers to the door into the earth that Abraham represented to God. Now that God had a door to mankind, we see that His favor and blessing flowed to His beloved creation who had been enslaved to the "earth curse." We find a great change in Abraham's life very quickly. In the very next chapter, we read that Abraham "had become very wealthy in livestock and in silver and gold." What happened? The earth curse had been overridden by the covenant! God's favor, or blessing, was legally on Abraham.

Have you ever wondered what Jesus meant when he quoted **Isaiah 61** in the temple (Luke 4)?

The spirit of the Sovereign Lord is on me, because the Lord has anointed me to preach good news to the poor?

He meant just what it says, or now man had a way to walk in the wisdom of God and a way to walk in life above the earth curse of Adam's day. A second Adam had come to bring a new order.

<u>Galatians 3:13</u>

Christ redeemed us from the curse of the law by becoming a curse for us, for it is written: "Cursed is everyone who is hung on a tree." He redeemed us (paid the price for us) in order that the blessing given to Abraham might come to the Gentiles through Christ Jesus, so that by faith we might receive the promise of the Spirit (life).

If we read passed the first verse of **Isaiah 61** that Jesus quoted in the temple, we would get a better understanding of what he meant by "good news for the poor."

<u>Isaiah 61:6</u>

You will feed on the wealth of nations and in their riches you will boast, instead of their shame (poverty) my people will receive a double portion, and everlasting joy will be theirs.

You see, Jesus paid the price for our son-ship. We are sons and daughters of the Most High God. **Galatians 4:1** reveals more concerning son-ship.

<u>Galatians 4:1</u>

What I am saying is that as long as the heir is a child he is no different than a slave, although he owns the whole estate. He is subject to guardians and trustees until the time set by his father. So also, when we were children, we were in slavery under the basic principles of the world. But when the time had fully come, God sent His son, born of a woman, born under law, to redeem those under the law, that we might receive the FULL RIGHTS of sons. Because you are sons, God sent the Spirit of His Son into our hearts, the Spirit who calls out, "Abba, Father." So you are no longer a slave, but a son; and since you are a son, God has made you also an heir.

We have an inheritance! The key point I want to make about an inheritance is that the blessing is never dictated by the receiver but by the one making the will. We do not have to receive from God by trying to earn points with Him. The will has already been declared and it is recorded in **Philippians 4:19**:

And my God will meet all your needs according to His glorious riches in Christ Jesus.

This scripture in Galatians gives us the insight we need to understand **Luke 6:20**:
Blessed are you who are poor, for yours is the kingdom of God (inheritance).

I always thought this verse was saying blessed are the poor—the poor darlings…someday they will die and go to heaven and then it will all be over. NO! It is saying the poor now have an avenue to the riches of God. THEY CAN HAVE THEIR NEEDS MET AND MUCH MORE! Jesus tells us in **Luke 6:38:**

Give and it shall be given to you, good measure, pressed down, RUNNING OVER…

This kingdom is one of abundance—blessings running over that you can't contain. Poverty is a curse, always has been a curse, and always will be a curse. God hates it! Jesus paid to redeem us from it.

Notes:

Chapter 5 What Does the Bible Say?

To get an accurate picture of God's view on debt and lack, we can look at the Old Testament. Israel had just come out of bondage in Egypt. God promised them a new land flowing with milk and honey, which meant that there would be plenteous provision for their needs. To enter into the blessing of God, Israel had to be strong and courageous and simply believe that God would bring His promises to pass. God gave His people a requirement for His blessing to come into their lives.

Deuteronomy 28:1

And it shall come to pass, if thou shalt harken diligently unto the voice of the Lord thy God, to observe and to do all his commandments which I command thee this day, that the Lord thy God will set thee on high above all nations of the earth: And these blessings shall come on thee and overtake thee, if thou shalt harken unto the voice of the Lord they God.

We can see a requirement in this scripture. Very simply, God's requirement was to diligently obey all of His commands. If the people obeyed this command, it was then God's responsibility (His good pleasure) to cause the blessing to come and overtake them. Remember, God had already decreed it; it was not something that He had to decide.

Deuteronomy 28:12

The Lord shall open unto thee His good treasure, the heaven to give the rain unto thy land in His season, and to bless all the work of thine hand: and thou shalt lend unto many nations, and thou shalt not borrow. And the Lord shall make thee the head, and not the tail; and thou shalt be above only, and thou shalt not be beneath; if that thou harken unto the commandments of the Lord thy God, which I command thee this day to observe.

Here we can see that God intended for Israel never to borrow, but they were to trust God, and He would provide great abundance for them to the extent that they could lend. They were never to be under another nation, but rather, to be on top. They were God's people.

In the second portion of Deuteronomy, we read the penalty for not observing the law of God. Israel would live under a curse (the earth curse), thus the blessing of God would not be theirs. It is vital that we understand God did not decide to curse them and judge them if they disobeyed. Rather, they came out of the covenant, out of the legal access that allowed God to bless them. Once they did this, then they stepped back into the earth curse, which as Genesis says, was a result of Adam's sin. If the people of God stayed under the covenant of God, then God says this in **Deuteronomy 28:8:**

The Lord will send a blessing on your barns and on everything YOU PUT YOUR HAND TO. The Lord will bless you in the land He is giving you.

Notice the people of Israel had a covenant of blessing. It was not the land itself. The land of Israel was ordinary land; but when they put their hands to it, the land was sanctified and blessed under their covenant with God. We must always remember that we have the blessing in us through Christ. It's not through some special job or place. So many of God's people are still looking for their promised land. My friend, you have the promises. Speak blessings no matter where you are right now. Those places and jobs are blessed because of the covenant that operates through you.

Deuteronomy 28:43
The alien who lives among you will rise above you higher and higher, but you will sink lower and lower. He will lend to you, but you will not lend to him. He will be the head, but you will be the tail.

The penalty for disobedience is the earth curse. If they broke covenant, Israel would need to borrow money and become slaves to other nations. Debt was listed as one of the curses Israel would have to live under if they did not fully obey (or have faith in) God. Disobedience would equal a complete reversal of the blessing of God.

The Word is clear. It is not God's plan for us to borrow our way through life. Remember, the Bible says that God does not change. Just because we live in America where debt is a way of life does not mean that God will change His principles and His Word on our behalf. It is we who have changed our practices from the Word of God. Borrowing our way through life is still a curse. We reap the consequences of slavery when we do not believe God or when we forsake His counsel.

Proverbs 22:7

The rich rule over the poor, and the borrower is servant to the lender.

Debt is not to be taken lightly. When we borrow, the Word says we become a slave to the lender. The borrower signs a contract promising labor to the lender. Interest on a debt is not just money. You can't go out to a tree and find money growing there. You must exchange hours of your life to obtain the money that you pay to the lender. **Proverbs 22:7** is very accurate. You become a slave when you go into debt.

1 Corinthians 7:23

You were bought with a price, do not become the slaves of men.

This scripture plainly reminds us that we were bought with the blood of Jesus. We are no longer our own. In that sense, we cannot legally give our labor to someone else because we are already owned. We must always remember that we have died with Christ in baptism. Dead men do not lust or seek after the things of life.

I am not saying that we should do without provision and wealth. I believe God wants to prosper us and give us the finer things of life. He delights in the prosperity of His servants. I am referring to our motives and priorities. Remember, God told Israel that the blessing would overtake them, meaning that the blessing was coming from behind them. It was not something they put in front of themselves as a focal point to be pursued. This would be idolatry.

Today, much of the debt we incur is birthed by idolatry. We must have possessions and status for whatever the cost. Debt hides the true cost of an item and sells you on a monthly payment. If you cannot live without something, chances are, you should.

Galatians 5:1

It is for freedom that Christ has set us free. Stand firm then, and do not let yourselves be burdened again by a yoke of slavery.

We are free! Do not let the world or the devil deceive you into thinking that you are not free or that God will not meet your needs, thus using debt. It is only through freedom that the Holy Spirit can move in your life to set others free. We need to make that freedom one of our priorities in life at all times.

Romans 13:8

Owe no man anything, but to love one another: for he that loveth another has fulfilled the law.

There are many scriptures that teach this principle. God never intended for His people to borrow their way through life, then or now. God is a jealous God. By leaning to debt as our source, we are trusting in or worshipping debt. If we will believe Him, the covenant we have will provide our needs today. **Hebrews 7:2** says that we have a better covenant than Israel possessed.

The Story of a Slave

When the Lord first began to deal with me about debt on a personal level, He told me that today's church is just like Israel–in slavery. Pharaoh held the people of Israel in slavery and forced them to make bricks to build his kingdom. In exchange for their work, he provided them with a place to sleep and food to eat. All of their labor went to Pharaoh. Today, this is most people's life story.

After they pay all of their creditors, the average family has just enough money left over to buy groceries. They do not own their house or their car that carries them to work. Many of the

After they pay all of their creditors, the average family has just enough money left over to buy groceries. They do not own their house or their car that carries them to work. Many of the expenses they pay in life are also related to working at their job, such as clothes, childcare, insurance, etc. So what do they get out of the deal? They have very little left to show for their labor. The families have become slaves producing profit for their lenders.

I hear this statement quite frequently, "We are just not getting ahead." I always answer back, "Why does that concern you? You are not supposed to worry about that. You are the slave in this relationship. As long as you are making your debt payments, then you are a good servant, and you should feel that you are pleasing your master." I know this sounds harsh, but I just want people to realize why they are not getting ahead. They have signed away most of their profit to the lenders.

Let me give you an illustration of my point. If you want to borrow $100,000 to buy a home at 10 percent interest, you have to earn $434,000 to pay back the $100,000 (taxes and interest included). To buy a $23,000 van, you will really pay $44,000 with taxes and insurance. As we examine the facts, it becomes quite obvious why we retire broke. Our lifetime is not long enough to give away so much money and still win financially. I want you to take a careful look at this next example and think about its implications. If you saved $1,000 per month for 7 years at 10 percent interest, you would have $120,959 saved at the end of that period. However, if you borrowed $120,959 at 10 percent interest and made the same $1,000 a month payment, it would **never be paid off** because the payment needed to pay off this size of a loan would be greater than $1,000. Did you read that carefully? Now do you see why 87 percent of American families retire below the poverty level?

If someone came into your house and stole all of your possessions, you would feel violated. Yet we go down to the local bank and sign away thousands of dollars and years of our life to the lender without blinking an eye. WE HAVE BEEN BRAINWASHED!

As Christians, we are called to be wise as serpents and harmless as doves. The Bible also says for us to be aware of the schemes of the enemy, Satan. Debt is one of those schemes that traps most of us. We need to flee from this snare and teach our children to do the same.

Kingdom Laws:
Sowing and Reaping

God has not left us here on earth hoping that we will somehow make it until we get to heaven. He has set laws and principles in the earth that will work in our favor. They can also work against us if we disregard them or rebel against them. Just because you might not know about the law of gravity doesn't mean that if you jump off the Empire State Building you will not be hurt. One of the key principles or laws that the Lord put into the earth was that of sowing and reaping. In the book of Genesis, the Lord says that there is seed-time and harvest-time and that this law will exist until the end. Every farmer knows this principle quite well–he depends on it.

This physical law in the natural realm is based on spiritual law. The principle of tithing and giving offerings is firmly established in the Word of God. You may think that tithing is only an Old Testament principle. Tithing did not pass away with the law. Tithing did not begin in the law! It was first mentioned when Abraham gave Melchizedek tithes on all the spoils of the battles in **Genesis 14:20**. Tithing is still a principle of God! Let's look a little deeper into this vital subject. We are going to spend some time here because it is essential for your deliverance.

The Sanctified Part: The Tithe

Most believers that I know view the tithe as a "have to"–something that God requires. They give it legally as a debt owed. They know that they *must* tithe. From this understanding–or I should say lack of understanding–they receive very little from their giving. First, we need to understand that the tithe is not *required* in the New Testament to be righteous before the Father. Notice, I said *required*–something that is law. No work of the flesh, even giving money, adds to the blood of Christ. The blood of Jesus set us free from the law and paid the <u>entire price</u> of our salvation. However the "law of the tithe" still exists and will be here until the earth passes away. The "law of the tithe" means a law or principle defining an unchangeable attribute of the kingdom of God in reference to the first fruits. We have laws in physics–although we did not invent them–that acknowledge an unchangeable aspect of the material world in which we live. So it is with this law of tithing.

The word *tithe* literally means "a tenth." In relation to giving the tithe, it means giving a tenth of one's income to the work of God, not just to anyone you choose. The Bible has specific guidelines concerning to whom it goes and for what purposes it serves.

As mentioned beforehand, the tithe did not originate with Moses and the law, although the tithe was indeed written into the law. It did not even originate with the story of Melchizedek, although that is the first place in the Bible the word *tithe* is used. The principle of the tithe is first seen in Genesis, the fourth chapter. Let's begin to read the story of Cain and Abel in **Genesis 4:2**:

Now Abel kept flocks, and Cain worked the soil. In the course of time Cain brought some of the fruits of the soil as an offering to the Lord. But Abel brought fat portions from some of the FIRST BORN of his flock. The Lord looked with favor on Abel and his offering, but on Cain and his offering he did not look with favor. So Cain was very angry, and his face was downcast. Then the Lord said to Cain, "Why are you angry? Why is your face downcast? IF YOU DO WHAT IS RIGHT, WILL YOU NOT BE ACCEPTED?"

Notice that the text says, "But Abel brought fat portions from some of the **first born** of his flock." The word "but" here is making a comparison of how Abel and Cain approached this offering. Many have taught that the problem with Cain's offering was that it was not a blood sacrifice. However, the Bible says that Cain worked the soil, not flocks. An offering can only be given from what someone owns, not from what he does not have. We know that meal or grain was accepted in the law for offerings, so we can assume that God would have received Cain's grain if it had been done the RIGHT way as the text says. What was right? What is the point the Bible makes when it mentions Abel's offering. We could ask, "What did Abel do right?" He gave fat portions (the best piece) from the FIRST BORN of the flock. Cain's offering is mentioned as being, "some of the fruits." The offerings revealed lordship.

From this story, I believe we see the principle of the tithe, or first fruits. This must have been taught to Cain and Abel by their parents, Adam and Eve. But why is the tithe or first fruits so important? Why wouldn't any old grain do for the offering?

Now we need to go back even farther to what I call legal access to the earth. Basically, Adam was given the dominion over the earth and was to care for it. Satan did not have legal authority–man did.

Luke 10:18

I [Jesus] saw Satan fall like lightning from heaven.

This must have been at a time before Adam was created. Satan rebelled against God and was cast from heaven. Revelation 12 further reveals that when Satan lost his position in heaven, he was cast to the earth.

Revelation 12:7

And there was war in heaven. Michael and his angels fought against the dragon, and the dragon and his angels fought back. But he was not strong enough, and they lost their place in heaven. The great dragon was hurled down–that ancient serpent called the devil, or Satan, who leads the whole world astray. He was hurled to the earth, and his angels with him.

One thing we know for sure–Satan was there in the garden trying to tempt Adam and Eve to believe him and doubt God. Why? He wanted to influence mankind–God's highest creation–and cause them to fall from God just as he had done. Satan knew that if he could convince man to sin, man would lose the position of authority over him, and he would rule over man through death. There was only one way for Satan to gain dominion over man and that was for man to rebel against God.

The only way for man to rebel involved the tree of the knowledge of good and evil. This tree was in the garden, and God commanded Adam and Eve not to eat from it. They could eat from any tree except from the tree of the knowledge of good and evil. You may ask why God put something that horrible in the garden in the first place. Indeed, the Bible does say that God planted the garden and the tree of the knowledge of good and evil. Was he trying to tempt man? No! **James 1:13** says it is impossible for God to tempt man with evil. There has to be another reason. I believe the answer is related to the same reason God did not stop Satan from being there.

Basically, Satan had a legal right to be there. He had no authority over the affairs of men, and he resented that man had authority over him; but he was there on the earth legally. God created man to rule the earth and subdue it. To do so meant that, sooner or later, man would have to deal with Satan, since Satan also wanted to rule over the earth. Man would be able to rule over Satan as long as he did so with the authority delegated to him by God. Remember that Hebrews 2 says man was created a little lower than the angels. Man's dominion came from the fact that God "placed everything under his [man's] feet," as it says in verse eight. God gave him the authority to rule over everything. God set a tree in the garden, which was off-limits to man. They were not to even touch it. When Satan deceived Eve into eating fruit from the tree, it ended the deep relationship between God and man. Now man's spirit became dark, and he lost the fellowship he had with God because he had chosen Satan to rule over him.

You may ask what this has to do with the tithe. It is important that you understand how Satan gained legal access to the affairs of men. It was through the same process that God had to regain legal access to man, and it was through that one tree that was placed in the garden–the tree of the knowledge of good and evil. It was a legal access point for Satan to gain entrance into the affairs of men. He had no authority over men until they ate the fruit. The tree was a kind of tithe or sanctified part. In other words, it was dedicated to God, and man's participation with it meant man had chosen disobedience and given Satan legal ground on which to stand. In the same way, when we choose to tithe, we are choosing God, and Satan cannot stop God from blessing us through that legal entry. As we study this out, you will see that the tithe is a legal access point for God to bless us.

An interesting scripture that shows us the authority that Satan gained over man is in **Luke 4:5** (Satan tempts Jesus).

The devil led him up to a high place and showed him in an instant all the kingdoms of the world. And he said to him, "I will give you all their authority and splendor, for IT HAS BEEN GIVEN TO ME, and I give it to anyone I want to. So, if you worship me, it will all be yours."

How did Satan gain possession of these kingdoms? He says they were given to him. Who gave them to him? Adam had authority over the earth, and he gave it to Satan in the garden. As we stated earlier, in order to give it back to man, God had to have legal access to the earth, which had to be through a man. Even after man repented for his error, God's own righteous law meant death (spiritual death) for the soul that sinned. This law of sin and death now operated in the earth and could not be broken. However, by tithing, man could open a legal doorway through which God could flow. The giving of the tithe sanctified man's provision so God could bless it. Satan could not accuse God of illegal entry since man still had dominion on the earth; and in fact, Satan, himself, had used man's authority to gain access in this same way. God must have taught this powerful principle of tithing to Adam so that he could still provide for him and so that Satan could not destroy him.

Let's read a passage in **Haggai 1:2** to better understand this truth.

This is what the Lord Almighty says: "These people say, 'The time has not yet come for the Lord's house to be built.'" Then the word of the Lord came through the prophet Haggai: "Is it a time for you yourselves to be living in your paneled houses, while this house remains a ruin?" Now this is what the Lord Almighty says: "Give careful thought to your ways. You have planted much, but have harvested little. You eat, but never have enough. You drink, but never have your fill. You put on clothes, but are not warm. You earn wages only to put them in a purse with holes in it."

Verse 9: *"You expected much, but see, it turned out to be little. What you brought home, I blew away. Why?" declares the Lord Almighty. "Because of my house, which remains a ruin, while each of you is busy with his own house. Therefore, BECAUSE OF YOU THE HEAVENS have withheld their dew and the earth its crops. I called for a drought..."*

You may say, "Wow, God is cruel. He called for a drought and wanted to hurt man." But I say God had to stop the flow of blessing because He had no legal access to bless man. They stopped tithing. The tithe was to go to the house of God and provide for the ministry, but these people were not putting God first. They weren't putting their money into the house of God, thus it was in shambles. The Lord told them it was happening because of them. He was basically saying, "You have legal dominion here, and you have cut me off from blessing you." The Lord told these people many times to give careful thought to **their** ways. In the second chapter, the Lord told them what would happen if they began to put God first.

Haggai 2:18

From this day on, from this twenty-fourth day of the ninth month, give careful thought to the day when the foundation of the Lord's temple was laid. Give careful thought: "Is there yet any seed left in the barn? Until now, the vine and the fig tree, the pomegranate and the olive tree have not borne fruit. FROM THIS DAY ON I will bless you."

What happened? We know that it was because of their ways that the curse (the earth curse) had been operating in their lives, so we also know it was because of their ways that the blessing of the Lord was able to flow to them again. What did they change? They laid the foundation of the Lord's house, and they tithed! Note the distinct moment in time when legal access was gained by God to bless them—when they started tithing.

Proverbs 3:9

Honor the Lord with your wealth, with the first fruits [tithe] of all your crops. Then your barns will be filled to overflowing and your vats will brim over with new wine.

Here we see the principle of the tithe again.

Romans 11:16

If the part of dough offered as first fruits is holy, then the whole batch is holy; if the root is holy, so are the branches.

The first fruit legally sanctifies the entire branch. We could say that the tithe makes the whole income blessed–holy and within God's legal domain.

When Malachi spoke about the people of Israel robbing God and how they were to return to God (fellowship restored legally), he said this:

Malachi 3:10

Bring the whole tithe [anything less would not work] into the storehouse, that there may be food in my house. 'Test me in this,' says the Lord Almighty, 'and see if I will not throw open the floodgates of heaven...'

Here we see that the tithe legally opens the "windows of heaven" to man. Please take special notice that the Bible says to bring the "whole tithe" into the storehouse. Here God gives specific advice concerning bringing the tithe. The whole tithe is required for the windows of heaven to open! People ask me all the time about the whole tithe. "Do I have to tithe on the gross or the net?" Well, you do not *have to* tithe at all. You *get to* tithe and share in the benefits of it. To step into this legal benefit of the heavens being opened, the whole tithe should be given.

Verse 11 says that if you tithe, God will prevent pests from devouring your crops and will cause your crops to flourish. Again, God could not stop Adam from sinning in the first place. **James 4:1** says, "We have not because *we* ask not." This is all because *we* have the legal dominion here on the earth. How does God have the legal right to rebuke Satan? We give Him that right when we tithe.

As we look back to Haggai, we see that once Israel began to put God first in their giving of the tithe, God was able to bless them, but they still had something else to do. They had to give offerings (something for God to multiply back to man) above the tithe, or you could say that we have to give something to God to bless once the windows of heaven are open. The tithe is a legal "door" of blessing–it opens the heavens. However, we are the ones who determine what comes out of heaven once it is open. The first thing that God asked Israel once they got the tithing problem fixed was if there was any seed left in the barn. They now had the right to be blessed in whatever they put their hand to. The blessing would be on their crops, and those crops would produce for them. Now that the windows of heaven were open, man still had control over the harvest he received based on the seed he planted. Many Christians do not understand this principle. They are tithing, but the overflow is not there. Well, how much seed are you planting?

Some people think that the offering and tithe are the same, but they are not. Malachi said that Israel was robbing God in both tithes and offerings. God made a note of the two different operations. Malachi said if man would operate in this law of God, then God would pour out a blessing that they would not be able to contain. Some people tithe but do not give offerings, and so they do not see the flowing that they want in their lives.

I hope you have a better understanding of this vital principle. It is very important you give in faith; you should not give just because you feel you have to or are bound by legalism.

Trusting the Kingdom Laws (releasing faith)

For years, I tithed and gave offerings, yet I continued to go backwards in my finances. I had no revelation in this area but gave legally, as a debt owed to God. I had many friends who were experiencing the same thing. Yet all I ever heard in church was that if I gave, God would take care of me. That is true, but the Lord showed me that the principle only works if I trust (release faith) in the right kingdom. Tithing is a principle of the Kingdom of God, not the world's kingdom. If I lean on the world's system, I will not see the fullest benefit of tithing. If I continually use debt (which steals from me) then I can't blame God for the holes in my purse. I put them there myself! When I give, it is the faith released and not the amount given that determines my harvest. I know I just shocked some folks, but let's look at this from the Word of God.

Mark 12:42

Jesus sat down opposite the place where the offerings were put and watched the crowd putting their money into the temple treasury. Many rich people <u>threw in large amounts</u>. But a poor widow came and put in two very small copper coins, worth only a fraction of a penny. Calling

His disciples to Him, Jesus said, "I tell you the truth, this poor widow <u>has put more into the</u> <u>*treasury then all the others.*</u> *They all gave out of their wealth: but she, out of her poverty, put in everything-all she had to live on."*

Jesus says here that many people were putting in large amounts of money, but a widow who put in a part of a penny gave more than all of them combined. How did she do that? The Bible says that the rich gave out of their excess. How much faith does it take to give out of your excess? Not much. However, the widow gave her all. She threw herself on God, and it took great faith. We see here that faith is the determining factor in our giving. It may take more faith for someone to give $5 than for another man to give $1,000. So you can see that if we are not releasing faith in our giving–even though we are giving–it does not profit us much. That is why it is so important to operate out of faith in everything that you do.

This principle is also clearly seen in the book of Judges. I believe the greatest danger debt poses is that it steals our tithe and our offerings. Usually, the first thing that goes out the window in the family budget is tithing and giving offerings. A farmer would know better, but we have not been taught these principles in most churches. In Judges, we find Israel held in bondage to Midian because of idolatry.

Judges 6:1
Again the Israelites did evil in the eyes of the Lord, and for seven years he gave them into the hands of the Midianites. Because the power of Midian was so oppressive, the Israelites prepared shelters for themselves in mountain clefts, caves and strongholds. <u>Whenever the Israelites planted their crops,</u> the Midianities, Amalekites and other eastern peoples invaded the country. They camped on the land and ruined the crops all the way to Gaza and did not spare a living thing for Israel.

Do you think Israel's problem was the fact that they did not believe in planting seed? No, it was not. The seed that Israel planted came to harvest just like the Lord promised. We know that it came to harvest because Gideon was in a winepress threshing wheat when the angel called him. He was hiding the grain from the Midianites. Israel's problem was that although they were planting seed and believing God for a harvest, <u>someone else was receiving the harvest on their seed.</u>

Today, most Christians who do tithe don't see the harvest on their seed because they are letting someone else receive the harvest on their seed (lenders). They are trusting in the world's system of finance (debt). Most act just like Gideon did when the angel approached him.

Judges 6:12

When the angel of the Lord appeared to Gideon, he said, "The Lord is with you, mighty warrior." "But sir," Gideon replied, "If the Lord is with us, why has all this happened to us? Where are all His wonders that our fathers told us about when they said, 'Did not the Lord bring us up out of Egypt?' But now the Lord has abandoned us into the hand of Midian."

The Lord never left Israel–Israel left the Lord. Gideon asked, "Why has all this happened to us?" Well, he should have known that Israel was not serving God anymore. He should have seen the idolatry in the land. His reply should have been something like, "Yes, Mr. Angel, I understand. I would have done the same thing if I were God. I knew that you would eventually humble Israel to the place of repentance." However, his reply was typical of most Christians. "Why is all this happening to me? Can't God see that I am in desperate need? Why has he left me?" All along, the reason for the mess was their own doing. God cannot help your situation until you repent from the error of your ways. It is only when you repent that you are open to receive the Word of God.

Judges 6:7

When the Israelites cried to the Lord because of Midian, he sent them a prophet...

This prophet told Israel the error of their ways. Israel repented and cried out to God for mercy, and God delivered them. It took faith for Gideon to follow the Lord's leading regarding their deliverance, and it will take faith for you to see God's hand at work as well. Let me make a bold statement: God will NOT deliver you until you repent and turn back to His Word! I know first-hand. We always want a miracle, but what we need is the Word of God. When we cry out for help, God's answer is His Word. It is by hearing the Word that faith comes, and faith is necessary for us to receive the help we need for the situations we face.

Again, the problem with Israel was not the fact that they did not plant seed. The same is true for most Christians. They will give tithes and offerings and still be in lack just like I was. The truth is, they have disobeyed the Word of the Lord, and they are living their lives according to the ways of this world (**Ephesians 2:1-3**). The fact that they are doing it in ignorance is no excuse. Hosea said that my people perish for lack of knowledge. The knowledge Hosea was referring to was the Word of God. If you are giving tithes and offerings and are still failing, it is because your trust is not in the principles of God. You are giving legally, bound by duty. The Bible says everything done without faith is sin (outside of God's kingdom). You are not releasing faith with your giving.

If you have debt and financial stress today, simply repent. Tell the Lord that you didn't understand and that you made a mistake. He will come to your aid and deliver you just like He did for me.

Another great passage of scripture that teaches the principle of giving is in 2 Corinthians. Paul was coming to collect a financial gift from the church in Corinth to take to another church. Before he got there he wrote:

2 Corinthians 9:6
Remember this: Whomever sows sparingly will also reap sparingly, and whomever sows generously will also reap generously. Each man should give what he has decided in his heart to give, not reluctantly or under compulsion, for God loves a cheerful giver.

Paul is asking them to remember. This means that he must have taught them the principle of sowing and reaping on occasion before this. He was reminding them of this powerful principle to stir their faith before he arrived. He was also reminding them of this principle not for the benefit of trying to get a big offering but for THEIR benefit. Many times, people say that all preachers want is their money. No, the Bible is plain about the benefit of giving. When Paul was talking to the

Philippian church regarding giving, he said, "Not that I am looking for a gift, but I am looking for what may be credited to <u>your account</u>."

2 Corinthians 9:10

Now He who supplies seed for the sower and bread for food will also supply and increase your store of seed and will enlarge the harvest of your righteousness. You will be made rich in every way so that you can be generous on every occasion.

Notice that God gives every man a seed to sow. This seed is different from the bread he is to eat. This seed is given for sowing. I believe tithing supplies our bread, and offerings (seed) increase our ability to give (overflow). Notice that God gives seed to those who will sow it. Then it says that God will increase the store and supply of seed. He didn't say bread. Bread rots and can't be stored for long. In the Lord's Prayer, Jesus prayed for the Father to give us this day our DAILY bread. But the seed is given for the purpose of sowing. How does God increase our store of seed? By us being faithful to plant the seed. According to the law of sowing and reaping, our seed will increase. Notice that as we are faithful to sow our seed, God will enlarge the harvest of our righteousness. What is the harvest? In the next verse we read that on EVERY occasion, we will be made rich so that we can be generous on EVERY occasion. The harvest is an overflow that we can use to bless others. In another verse of that chapter, Paul states it well.

2 Corinthians 9:13

<u>Because of the service by which you have proved yourselves</u>, men will praise God for the obedience that accompanies your confession of the gospel of Christ, and for your generosity in sharing with them and with everyone else.

Paul makes it clear that this is one of the key responsibilities of the church, and each of us is required to prove ourselves in this area. The greatest danger in using debt as a way of life is that it tempts or forces you to eat your seed as bread. If you eat your seed as bread, you will not see an increase in your storehouse, and you will not be able to be generous on every occasion. Planting seed is not the only key. As I said earlier, if you have holes in your purse (by not tithing) then the increase will never stay there long enough for you to plant it to get more. If you stop the thief from stealing your seed and you begin to sow, watch out! You will see the power of God move on your behalf to increase your store of seed.

Paul made this principle clear in **Ephesians 4:28**:

He who has been stealing must steal no longer, but must work, doing something useful with his own hands, that he may have something to SHARE with those in need.

Why didn't Paul just tell the guy who was stealing to stop stealing and work for a living with his own two hands? Paul knew the principle of sowing and reaping. If the guy would begin to sow, Paul knew that his life would truly be changed and that his needs would always be met.

After a radio talk show one day, a lady called me and asked me if I believed in tithing. I said, "Yes, Ma'am." She asked, "Do you believe in tithing on the gross or the net pay?" I replied, "Well, it depends on who is more important–God or the government." She got a little upset and said, "I can't do that, I am barely getting by now." So I asked, "Do you have any debt payments?" She replied, "Of course I do." I then asked her if she would be able to tithe if she had no debt payments. She replied, "Of course I would." That is the state of most Christians. Debt has put them in a very precarious situation. They desperately need to plant seed to increase their harvest, but they have no seed left to plant. Another verse which promises a return on our giving is **Luke 6:38**:

Give, and it will be given to you, a good measure, pressed down, shaken together and running over, will be poured into your lap. For with the measure you use, it will be measured to you.

You cannot get away from this truth. God is holding you responsible to give Him something that He can multiply back to you. It is not too late to start over if you have blown it. Let's face it, we all have. Israel blew it, and God was always ready to forgive them and restore their fortunes.

Psalms 126:4

Restore our fortunes, O Lord, like streams in the Negev. Those who sow in tears will reap with songs of joy. He who goes out weeping carrying seed to sow, will return with songs of joy, carrying sheaves with him.

Many times in my life, when I have not had enough to meet the pending bill, I had enough for a seed, so I would give it away. God always made a way and took care of the need. It takes faith to step out on God's Word, but once you test it and find that it works every time, you will find yourself becoming stronger and stronger. Then the next time you face a need that looks hopeless, you can smile, knowing that it will be supplied.

Giving requires faith! A farmer plants his seed in the ground by faith, trusting the natural law of sowing and reaping. He takes a large bin of seed, which has value and could meet his temporary need, and he sows it into the soil. The seed totally disappears from his sight. In reality, he has lost it. He can never go back out and gather it up again if he changes his mind. He does not even know how that seed will turn into a live, thriving plant. But he trusts that it will–and it does. The same is true about sowing financial seed. To let go of something in your hand that you've worked hard to get takes faith in the law of sowing and reaping. After you have done it and have tasted the fruit of the harvest, you will always be willing to plant with an expectant faith!

Chapter 7 No One Can Serve Two Masters

Matthew 6:24

No one can serve two masters. Either he will hate the one and love the other, or he will be devoted to the one and despise the other.

You Cannot Serve BOTH God and Money!

When I was growing up, I always thought this scripture dealt with what I adored or admired. I knew that I loved God, so I assumed that I would never try to serve two masters. However, one day the Lord showed me that I–along with many of his children–had indeed done this. The definition of *serve* in Webster's Dictionary is "to be a servant, give service, work, and perform duties." Apparently, the word *serve* pertains to my actions or labor. Who was I serving? I had to repent before the Lord.

Many Christians are seeking the things of the world and the success it has to offer. God is a God of success, but the question is what motivates and drives us? Remember that you will always serve what you believe to be your source. The Bible says that the pagans run after the things of life (money) because they think that money is their answer. If you think that money is your answer, you will base your decisions on money. As children of God, we are not to be led in life by money but rather by where our Father leads us.

Many people are not where they are supposed to be in life because they have followed money instead of serving God with their whole heart. An easy way to find out where your trust lies is to ask yourself how much time you really spend in the Word and in prayer. Our priorities are clearly evident when we look at our actions.

Matthew 6:33

But seek first His kingdom and His righteousness, and all these things will be given to you as well.

This reveals a major key to prospering in the kingdom of God. Why was Abraham so wealthy? He was willing to sacrifice Isaac, trusting God all the way. He was willing to give God his most valued possession in life. God knew that He had Abraham's heart, so He could trust Abraham with wealth.

Solomon also chose God when asked what he wanted from God. He did not ask for his own gain but for wisdom to rule God's people. God rewarded him with both. The Bible is full of men and women who chose to believe God in the times of testing, and God delivered and prospered them.

Deuteronomy 30:14

The Word is very near you; it is in your mouth and in your heart so you may obey it. See, I set before you today life and prosperity, death and destruction. For I command you today to love the Lord your God, to walk in His ways, and to keep His commands, decrees, and laws; then you will live and increase, and the Lord your God will bless you in the land you are entering to possess.

Remember, it is your choice; God has already given you the victory. The Bible says our faith gives us the victory. Faith in what? As the verse above says: we must have faith in God's desire and ability to fulfill His word on our behalf. The choice is YOURS!

Chapter 8

Faith and Patience: God's Promotion System

Every time I sit down with couples at their kitchen tables, I wish I had hours to share with them a word that will change their lives–the word of faith! For years, I thought I did have faith, but in a crisis I found nothing to hold me. I was very weak. I would waver–wondering whether God would answer my cry. I assumed that God was sovereign, and I would just have to wait and see what God did in any particular case. The fact is that God is sovereign, but He cannot violate His Word. When I began to learn faith, my life changed.

Faith is simply believing what God said is true. No questions asked. If God said it, I believe it, and the issue is settled. So many Christians rationalize the scripture to fit what they think God meant instead of just believing God. Trusting in God's Word is something you learn to walk in. Not only did David have faith in God's ability to deliver Goliath into his hands through the covenant, but he also had faith because he had tested that covenant with the bear and the lion. He had found it to be solid. Most Christians are not confident in God's will for them, thus faith cannot be released.

1 John 5:14

This is the confidence we have in approaching God; that if we ask anything according to His will, He hears us. And if we know that He hears us–whatever we ask–we know that we have what we asked for.

If we ask anything according to the will of God, we can have confidence that we have received. We must know the will of God, which is the Word of God, to know that we have received. A prayer of hope with a 'maybe' attitude is not faith.

James 4:1

What causes fights and quarrels among you? Don't they come from your desires that battle within you? You want something but don't get it. You kill and covet, but you cannot have what you want. You quarrel and fight. <u>*You do not have, because you do not ask God.*</u>

This is the verse that I teach every family I see. When you need something, ask God for it in faith, and then wait for Him to bring it or give you direction on how to get it. Most families I see use their credit card, and ***then*** they ask God to pay for it. I did that for years, and I found that it didn't work very well.

Faith has a definition. If I ask God for a washing machine and someone gives me an iron, I would not say that God has supplied my need. Yet people will ask the Lord for something, and then when it doesn't show up right away, they grab the credit card and figure that using the card must be God's answer. I used to thank God for credit, but now I know better. Jesus said all things are possible for them that believe. Every time He healed someone, He said, "Your faith has made you well." When His disciples were fearful in the boat during the storm, He rebuked them and said they were of small faith.

I have learned to use faith for the things I need. I am not saying that a raven will bring you a new car and you are to sit around drinking sodas, waiting for the car to show up. We are to do all that we can do, and then stand. He may have someone give you the thing you need, or He may show you where to buy it at a reduced cost or even provide it in a most unusual way.

One of the most unusual ways God provided for us was when our daughter wanted a pair of Mickey Mouse roller skates. At the time, we did not have the money for them, so we told her to pray and believe God for them. About a month later, my wife's father bought a used car at an auction. In the trunk was a pair of Mickey Mouse skates; my daughter got what she believed.

Mark 11:24

Therefore I tell you, whatever you ask for in prayer, believe that you have received it, and it will be yours.

This is the verse that has changed my life and healed my body. For two and a half years, I suffered from severe mental and emotional problems due to a disorder called hypoglycemia. I had been to the hospital many times, but there was no cure except to change my diet. I had a very hard time trying to watch what I ate. After receiving prayer one evening, I did not feel any different and could still sense the same symptoms, even though the anointing was heavy.

During the night, I had a short dream during which the above scripture was quoted. In the morning, I kept thinking about this scripture, yet I did not know where to find it. After some searching, I finally found it. I had been trying to confirm the Word of God through the circumstances or lack of symptoms. I realized from the dream that I received by faith, and faith is the evidence of things not seen. So instead of becoming discouraged, I began to thank God for my healing before I saw it, based on His Word. From the moment I received my healing by faith, the symptoms disappeared and have not been back.

Notice the two verb tenses in Mark 11:24. I am to believe that I receive <u>when I pray</u>, and then it WILL be mine. This is the key. Faith does not wait to have proof that the answer is at hand. Faith knows that the answer is there when I need it.

Remember, Israel received manna and water each day in the wilderness by faith. The Bible says that the righteous will walk by faith and not by sight. We are to be no different. God requires you and me to believe Him and walk by faith as well. I learned to believe that I actually receive my request when I pray. I have learned to keep a record of the date and the thing I need. From that day on, I thank God for the answered prayer. By faith, I have the need met.

Hebrews 11:1
Faith is the substance of things hoped for, and the evidence of things not seen.

Philippians 4:6
Do not be anxious about anything, but in everything, by prayer and petition, with thanksgiving, present your requests to God. And the peace of God, which transcends all understanding, will guard your hearts and your minds in Christ Jesus.

I present my needs to God in prayer, with thanksgiving, because I know He does not lie, and He will honor His Word. The peace of God is mine because I KNOW that the thing that I have put before Him is done, even though I see no change. If I didn't believe that it was done, I would still be anxious and would lack peace.

Jesus taught one of the most powerful parables about faith in the Bible in **Luke 8:4-15**. The parable of the sower is a well-known story, but most of my life, I never really knew what it meant. Jesus explained it in verses 11-15.

This is the meaning of the parable: The seed is the Word of God. Those along the path are the ones who hear, and then the devil comes and takes away the Word from their hearts, so that they cannot believe and be saved. Those on the rock are the ones who receive the Word with <u>joy</u> when they hear it, but they have no root. They believe for a while, but in the time of testing they fall away. The seed that fell among thorns stands for those who hear, but as they go on their way they are choked by life's worries, riches and pleasures, and they do not mature. But the seed on good soil stands for those with noble and good hearts who hear <u>the word, RETAIN it, and by persevering, produce a crop.</u>

Here is another key—retain the Word. When the Word is sown and is believed, joy comes. If you are sick and you receive the word that Jesus will heal you, joy comes. Joy is always a companion of faith.

The Word you are standing on will be tested, not by God, but by the devil. He knows that the Word of God cannot return void, but it will produce what it was sent to produce. The devil will try to get that Word out of you. If he can't break your faith with buffeting, he will then try to draw you off of the Word to follow your own wants and desires. If he can't shake you and you RETAIN the Word, it WILL produce what you have believed!

The "fight of faith" is simply fighting to stay in faith. Many times, there is a period of time between when we believe we receive and when the manifestation appears. Once, Daniel questioned an angel about why it had taken so long for him to show up after Daniel had prayed. The angel said that he had been dispatched at the MOMENT Daniel prayed, but he had to wrestle with the Prince of Persia for 21 days to get there. Many times, God is working on our behalf, and we just cannot see it. That is why the Bible says that through faith and patience, we inherit the promises.

Faith is the key that unlocks the door, and patience is the means of getting the goods to you. Most immature Christians lack patience. When their faith is tested with circumstances that contradict the Word, they grow weary and become double-minded. Then they receive nothing from God. The Bible says that patience has a great reward. If you do not learn to use faith and patience, you will always be at the mercy of the devil's schemes and the world's system. Using faith is a powerful tool in helping you stay out of debt and having your needs met. It is also the most exciting way to live.

"I always say it is better to have a testimony than a debt payment!"

Notes:

Chapter **9** Which Kingdom?

Families I've consulted with have asked me over and over again where they have missed it. Though they were Christians, they were not seeing the promises of God revealed in their lives concerning God meeting their needs. Instead, they were finding hard times and stress as a constant companion. When I was in serious debt myself, experiencing great turmoil in my life as a result of debt, I had to ask myself the same question. Why wasn't God honoring His Word on my behalf? When I began to seriously seek God with this question, He began to show me the answer. He let me know that I had placed my faith in the world's system instead of in His system.

Jesus spoke constantly about the Kingdom of God. He contrasted this kingdom with the world's kingdom many times. He said strange things like, "If you want to be great in this new kingdom, you must be the least," and "If you want to find your life, you must lose it." These commands were in direct conflict with the world's kingdom. He was talking about a new way of life–a new kingdom. Every kingdom is built upon rules of conduct and priorities. He was saying that the rules of this world's kingdom do not work in the new kingdom He was proclaiming. To live at peace in the kingdom of God, we are to walk by the laws that govern the kingdom.

Ephesians 2:1

And you were dead in your trespasses and sins, in which you formerly walked according to the course of this world...

Before we came to the Lord, we lived fully in the world's kingdom with all of its rules of conduct and priorities. This world's kingdom is ruled by greed and selfishness. But the kingdom of God is not a matter of eating and drinking, but of righteousness, peace, and joy in the Holy Ghost (**Romans 14:17**). Life is more than just fulfilling our fleshly desires; a spiritual side of life is revealed in the new kingdom. Concern for others and giving to others become rules to live by, instead of always taking care of the big "I."

In the new kingdom there is provision for our needs, but we are not to seek them in the sense of living for their fulfillment. Now we are to "Seek first His kingdom and His righteousness, and all these things (we need) shall be added to us." (**Matthew 6:33**) What does it mean to seek first His kingdom?

Romans 12:2

And do not be conformed to this world, but be transformed by the renewing of your mind, that you may prove what the will of God is, that which is good, and acceptable, and perfect.

Seeking first His kingdom means we are first concerned about the kingdom business. We need to spend time learning the rules for this new kingdom, as well as how it operates. Our minds have been trained in the world's system, so we need to renew our minds with the Word of God to the new kingdom's operations of the Spirit. By doing so, we will know the will of God, and we will find true peace and fulfillment. The more time we spend studying this new kingdom, the more freedom we will find!

John 8:31

Jesus therefore was saying to those Jews who had believed Him, "If you abide in My word, then you are truly disciples of Mine; and you shall know the truth, and the truth shall make you free."

Again, we see that the more we know the Word, the more our minds will be renewed to this new kingdom, and the result will be freedom.

Jesus knew we were a needy people, and he spent much time teaching His disciples how the new kingdom worked with regard to meeting our earthly needs. In Matthew 6, Jesus taught one of His greatest teachings on this new kingdom. Jesus made it clear that we are not to worship the treasures of this life. At the same time, He made it clear that we have needs and that God has made provision for those needs. Jesus called anyone who is anxious about natural needs a "person of little faith." He explained how the heathen (those who are under this world's system) spend time and energy to pursue their needs and wants. In the Kingdom of God, we do not have to run after our needs like the ungodly. Instead, He indicates that God Himself will add and bring to our lives those things we need.

James teaches us in chapter 4 and verse 1 that we do not have the things we need because we do not ask God for them. I have come to the conclusion that the reason we do not ask God for our needs is because we do not have faith that God will take care of them. If we truly knew that God would take care of our needs, we would run to Him with them. I have heard many Christians say that they didn't want to bother God with the trivial affairs of life. This, my friend, is a doctrine of the devil. God will move heaven and earth to fulfill His Word on your behalf if you will only believe. Again, Jesus said we were not to worry about the things we eat and the clothes we wear. The only way to avoid worrying about these things is to <u>know</u> that it is God's will for you to have these things, and He will give you those things when you believe Him.

In America, we have proven to our satisfaction that the world's system of meeting our needs works. We give the store a piece of plastic and fully expect to receive the item we want. This is faith. Unfortunately, many Christians have developed faith in this system to a greater degree than faith in the Word and its ability to supply our needs. I found this to be my problem. I would agree with the Word when it said that God would meet my needs, but I felt that God would always use the methods of this worldly kingdom to do so. I now realize that I was wrong.

The Van Story

The rules of this earthly kingdom do not work the same way as the principles of the kingdom of God. Many Christians are frustrated with their lives because they are trying to live in two kingdoms at the same time. I will tell you right now that *you cannot do it*. My wife and I became so desperate in our financial situation that we finally asked ourselves if we were doing something wrong. The Lord showed us that we were leaning on our ability to obtain credit to meet our needs instead of leaning on the Word of God. We repented to the Lord for this, and we made a vow that we would not lean on debt as long as we lived. At the time we made that commitment, we had no money, and we were behind on about every bill. The phone calls from creditors woke us every morning. Even though we knew of no natural way out of our situation, we believed that God was able.

A few days after we made that commitment, I was driving our well-used van on a visitation call. The person I was visiting was a mechanic. When he saw smoke billowing out of it when I started the engine, he asked to have a look inside the hood. After checking the engine, he informed me that I had a broken head gasket and that I needed to drive it home, park it and have it fixed. He didn't know that I had no extra money. He didn't know that I had a bill due in three days for $1,600 that I didn't have one dollar saved to pay. On the way home from that visit, I was discouraged to say the least. I began to tell the Lord that I didn't know what to do. I told Him that I could not sell a broken van, and I could not afford to fix it. In my frustration and desperation, I told God that it might just be better for the van to burn up. When I pulled into my office parking lot and turned the key off, the van burst into flames! There were flames rising seven feet off of the hood, and I just sat there in awe. *Whoa God, you heard what I said*, I thought to myself. Finally, it hit me that I had better get out of the burning van! For some reason, it took the fire department a very long time to get to me, despite the fact that they were only five doors down the road, and so the van was totally charred by the time the flames were doused. I was stunned and relieved. The insurance company settled the claim, paying off the van and leaving me with enough left over to pay my $1,600 debt. I was grateful for divine deliverance. However, I now had a need that had to be met–I needed a vehicle.

My father heard about my van burning up and wanted to take me out to look for a new one. I was too embarrassed to tell him that I had no money, so I went with him to look anyway. I was so desperate that I secretly hoped he would offer to buy me one. Of course, I found a van that I liked, and my father offered me $5,000 toward the purchase. That sounded great, but that left me with $12,000 to finance. I applied for the loan and was approved, but that night I was in turmoil. The Lord's direction was clear, "Do not go into debt, but trust me." I decided to turn down the bank's offer, and I thanked my dad but told him that I just couldn't go into debt. To make a long story short, someone gave us a car to drive. We worked and saved our money, and in a year and a half we paid cash for a two-year-old van.

This was our first experience with trusting God for our needs in a big way. Now we pay cash for new cars, and God prospers us as we put Him first and trust Him. God has proven Himself faithful. We have lived with our needs met ever since we made that commitment to walk in His kingdom!

Hebrews 11:1

Faith is the substance of things hoped for and the evidence of things unseen.

Faith is the currency of this new kingdom. All of the resources of heaven are yours, but they are only accessed by faith. I taught my kids to replace the word "things" with their need. So they say, "Faith is the substance of the 'new bike' hoped for and the evidence of the 'new bike' unseen." I have found this to be helpful, even for adults.

A fact that shocks many believers is that God is not moved by need alone. Many times when I was in despair, I would wonder why God was not doing something to help me. God could not do anything to help until I had faith for it. Jesus could not do many good things in His hometown because of unbelief. Unbelief stops the power and provision of God. Israel could not enter the Promised Land because of unbelief.

Make a decision that from this point on you will be a believer and a receiver of all that God has for you. To do that, you must spend time in the Word of God. Faith comes from the Word, and with your faith comes the victory.

Make a commitment to not use debt as a way of life, but wait on the Lord for direction. Base your life on the Kingdom principles, and you will win.

1 Peter 5:7

Cast your care on Him for He cares for you!

To cast my care on God, I must know that God cares for me and that His concern for me never changes. How do I cast my care on the Lord?

Philippians 4:6

Do not be anxious about anything, but in everything, by prayer and petition, with thanksgiving, present your requests to God. And the peace of God, which transcends all understanding will guard your hearts and your minds in Christ Jesus.

The answer is prayer. When I am anxious about something, I can take it to the Lord and give that care to Him. When I come to Him, I must believe what **Hebrews 11:6** says.

Without faith, it is impossible to please God, because anyone who comes to Him must believe that He exists and that He rewards those who earnestly seek Him.

I must be confident that He will reward my faith because of what He has promised in His Word. Many people think that they must cry and carry on, and somehow God will see that their situation is serious and take note of it. Some feel that the more people there are praying for their situation, the greater chance of getting God's attention. Some feel that if they can pray long enough or fast long enough or do enough good works, God will notice. My friend, only faith pleases God.

Matthew 6:7

And when you pray, do not keep on babbling like pagans, for they think they will be heard because of their many words. DO NOT BE LIKE THEM, for your Father knows what you need before you ask Him.

Jesus is saying that begging and praying long prayers are not how the kingdom of God works. God knows your need before you ask. You do not need to convince Him of your need. You simply need to know how to pray and receive those things you need. Jesus then goes on and teaches us how we should pray to get results.

Matthew 6:9

This then, is how you should pray:

"Our Father in heaven, hallowed be Your name, Your kingdom come, Your will be done on earth as it is in heaven. Give us this day our daily bread. Forgive us our debts, as we also have forgiven our debtors. And lead us not into temptation, but deliver us from the evil one."

Here Jesus gives the famous "Lord's Prayer." I was taught to quote this scripture as a young boy. In the church where I grew up, we quoted this scripture every Sunday, but we didn't have understanding. Jesus was not giving us a prayer to quote. He was teaching us how to pray effectively and have our needs met. He taught us that first we come through the name of the Father, for that is our legal access to heaven's storehouses.

The Bible says in **Hebrews 1:4**:

So He became as much superior to the angels as the name He has inherited is superior to theirs.

We come to the Father in the name of Jesus. Next, Jesus taught us that we are to pray the will of heaven into the earth. We are heaven's agents here on earth. Unless we pray the will of God (the Word) into the earth, it will not be loosed here.

Matthew 16:19

I will give you the keys (authority) of the kingdom of heaven; whatever <u>you bind on earth</u> will be bound in heaven, and whatever <u>you loose on earth</u> will be loosed in heaven.

Notice that Jesus said *we* have the keys of the kingdom. The key to heaven is our binding or loosing on the earth, and heaven will back up what we do. As a believer, only you have the keys to heaven, and only you can loose those resources into your life (on earth).

James 4:1

You have not because you ask not.

Unless you ask, heaven cannot come into the earth. Again, the issue is legal access to the earth through a man.

You loose heaven when you pray the prayer of faith regarding the will of heaven (the Word). Many believers are frustrated and angry with God for not helping them, but you see, we have the key. God does not have the key (authority) to bring heaven into earth without a man.

Besides loosing heaven on the earth, we are to bind the enemy from causing destruction in the earth. We are to cast out demons and heal the sick. If we do not use our authority over Satan, no one else can. This truth will change our lives if we understand it. Instead of just putting up with things, we can bind the operation of the kingdom of darkness in our lives. Instead of doing without what we need for living life to the fullest, we can loose the resources of heaven in our lives.

Remember: The only heaven you will experience is the heaven you grasp by faith and loose into your life.

Chapter 10 The Economy of God

As you probably know by now, the economy of God is different than the economy of the United States. The world's economy can fail and go into depression or even collapse, but the economy of God can never fail. As we discussed in the last chapter, the economy of God does not use money but rather faith as its currency.

Philippians 4:19

And my God will meet all your needs according to His glorious riches in Christ Jesus.

I am glad that Paul said my needs are met according to what heaven has and not by what my kingdom has in it. Many people make the mistake of limiting themselves by their own potential, by what they see around them, or by their past. But thank God that I have a greater kingdom from which to draw. Many people have quoted Philippians 4:19 not realizing that Paul wrote that verse in response to a gift that the church sent to him. He was telling them that by giving into the kingdom, they had a right to draw out of the kingdom and have all their needs met.

Maybe things are not going well in your business, or your income is not where you desire. Be of good courage! Jesus will lead you to green pastures, and your needs will be met. In the church I pastor, I teach the Word of God regarding getting needs met. I was a little concerned when time and again people would come to me and tell me that they had been tithing and giving offerings and speaking the Word over their life regarding increase; and then, much to their surprise, they would lose their job. This happened over and over again. At first, I was confused. But as I saw these same people start their own businesses or get better jobs, I understood that things change when you believe God. **You are not limited by where you came from but by where you are going.**

I remember when I was in debt, and creditors would call us in the mornings. It was a bad time—a time of discouragement. As I began to take heed to the Word of God, hope began to rise in me, but the mountain still seemed so big. I just could not see a way out. I remember the night that my wife woke me up and said the Lord had spoken to her and told her we would be in ministry helping families get out of debt. This was long before I was a pastor, and I did not receive that word very well. Actually, I was angry about it. I told her to go back to bed. "Why doesn't God tell us how to get out of debt first?" I asked in disgust.

I was not in a very good mood in those days. My wife kept praying for me, and I kept getting stronger in my faith walk. At the time, we had ten maxed-out credit cards, three finance company loans, $32,000 in personal debt to family members, various smaller debts, $14,000 in back taxes and a small pile of medical bills. Besides all the debt, my income was not very good.

Slowly, the Word began to come alive to me, and I started to see that God was my only hope. I began to see my mistakes and how I had gotten myself into trouble, so I stopped blaming God. I then repented to the Lord for my mistakes and my rebellious attitude, and He began to lead me out of our wilderness situation.

About six months after my wife told me what the Lord had shown her concerning our future, God gave me a dream in which I saw I was to shut down my other business. I obeyed, and we launched Faith-Full Family Finances while we were still in debt. The Lord encouraged us that as we went and proclaimed the good news of the gospel that we would come out of debt ourselves. As we were obedient to go forth, we paid all of our debts off in two and a half years. Then we saved over $100,000 in cash within the next three years. We were thrilled! We had found that God's Word works. Eventually, we paid cash for 55 acres of land and built our dream home.

Those who have seen our deliverance know that it was God. Since then, God has used us to reach thousands of families with this message of freedom. Our lives have truly been changed, and we will praise the living God forever.

Proverbs 10:22

The Blessing of the Lord brings wealth and He adds no sorrow with it.

Truly, the Lord has delivered us. There is no way that I can take any credit for what has happened to my family. I do know that God does not favor anyone over another. What He said He will do, He will do for you.

Deuteronomy 8:18

Remember the Lord your God, for it is He who gives you the power to produce wealth, and so confirms His covenant.

The covenant we walk in is a covenant of blessing. The fact that God wants to prosper His children confirms His covenant and faithfulness. Let's face it. God meeting your need is a sign to unbelievers that the God you serve is the true and living God.

You may remember movies you have seen that show a tribe of natives worshipping idols. If you will take note, most of these idols are gods of nature. These people depend on idols to meet their needs, hoping that these gods will cause the rains to come in season and their herds to multiply. If our God does not meet our needs, then those watching our lives can proclaim that our God is no more powerful than theirs.

I always tell people that their bounced checks will not witness to their banker about the gospel. God is a God of integrity. He tells us not to bring reproach upon His name. The Word clearly tells us that it is God's will to meet our needs.

I remember when we still lived in Tulsa. I was jogging one day, and the Lord spoke to me and told me to sell my home and move back to Ohio. I was so excited when I got home to share with my wife what the Lord had said. Things were tough in Tulsa. There was a major oil recession going on, and since Tulsa's economy had a large oil base, it meant hard times for most people. To say we were not sad at the thought of leaving Tulsa is an understatement. Our income had been dropping, and things were very tight. We were having trouble making our house payment.

I went to the bank and told them that we would be moving and asked if there was anything we could work out until the house sold. Without saying too much, the loan officer asked us to step in a side room where there was a table with hundreds of cards on it. She said every card represented a foreclosure, and she did not want another one. She told us that the bank would accept one half of our regular house payment for a period of up to six months. The house had to sell in that six-month period of time, or we would have to pay back the rest of the payments. If we could not do it, the bank would foreclose. Well, that all sounded great to us. It was more than we had hoped for. There was just one more small catch concerning selling the house that we needed to discuss. We owed $10,000 more on our house than it was worth, due to the recession. The banker thought about our dilemma, then she said she would accept whatever the house appraised for as the full pay-off price. Additionally, if the house sold, our credit report would still reflect a good standing with the bank. We could not believe this! We did not even know that banks would do such things. We were so thrilled that our deliverance was underway. We just knew that God would bring the buyer quickly, and we would be on our way.

We knew something was wrong when after five months not one person had called or come by the house to see it. The real estate agent told us that everyone was trying to move out of Tulsa, so there were hundreds of homes on the market. We only had one month to go until our deadline. I started to get a little nervous, knowing that I did not have the money to make up the six half payments. Our income had dropped now to the point where we were even having trouble making the reduced payment.

With two weeks left, no one had called. After praying, we decided to list the home ourselves. We figured we could do just as good a job selling our home as the real estate company was doing. The owner of the company agreed to let us out of our contract with two weeks left on our deadline from the bank. We placed an advertisement in the Tulsa Sunday paper and prayed.

We had one call, and it was from a single woman who was looking for a home that sounded just like ours. After looking at the home, she decided to buy it. Oh, I cannot tell you how relieved I was. The amazing thing about her purchase was that she had cash! We realized what a miracle this was! To obtain a mortgage would have taken more than three weeks to process, and we would have missed the bank deadline. I will never forget the look on the banker's face when we brought her the cash to pay that loan off. Literally, her mouth fell open, and she asked, "Where did you find that buyer?" We told her we didn't—God did. God will always meet your needs. It may not be how you would do it, but God is never late. His provision is always abundantly more than you could have done in your own strength.

Ephesians 3:20

And now God is able to do exceeding abundantly above all you can ask or think.

Chapter 11 Getting Started

I hope this material has helped you gain spiritual insight into the snare and stronghold debt brings to people's lives and the freedom that God's Word can bring to those who believe. When I work with families, they usually assume that if I can help them work out their budget problems, then they will have it made. Many wonder why I spend so much time dealing with the spiritual side of debt. The answer is simple. If I help a family gain control of their finances from a numbers perspective only, I have not changed the root of the problem. The heart is where our decisions are based and where the direction of our lives is set. The lust for things and the pride of life are spiritual issues that must be dealt with. If I do not deal with them, then the family will go right back into debt after I have shown them how to get out.

However, everything in life is not spiritual. Once the spiritual side of debt is addressed, we need to utilize sound financial principles to prepare a plan to eliminate all debt as quickly as possible. After working with thousands and thousands of families, we have found that the average family can be out of debt in five to seven years, including their mortgage, usually without changing their income. I know that sounds incredible, but it is true. We must always remember the incredible power of money and compound interest. The lender knows these principles thoroughly and uses them against the consumer. By understanding these laws of compound interest, we can use them to our advantage.

I have been in debt, and I am now free–being free is better! The memory of the stress I once lived under makes me cringe. I give all the glory to Jesus for delivering me from the snare of the enemy. You may be reading this book and you may still be in the snare. Let me assure you that the principles laid out here have worked for many. God is no respecter of people. What he did for me, He will do for you.

Notes:

 **Chapter** **12**

The Steps to Freedom

The very first step to becoming debt free is to list every debt you owe. This includes all medical bills and personal debts to friends and family. Please take time now to list them all. Every home has a drawer filled with bills that we do not like to face, but we are not going to look at this problem with a fear mentality, but with faith. By faith, we see all these bills paid in full! After you list all of your bills, it is important that you fill out the budget page in order to balance the budget. This is so you can determine whether or not there are shortages.

Whom I Owe	Interest Rate	Balance Owed	Payment

Total Debt Owed $_____ Total Payments being made $_____

Now that you have faced the bill drawer and you know exactly what you owe and where your budget is, you are ready to go onto the next step. Obviously, the next step in debt elimination is finding the money needed to pay the debt off, but that is where most people stop because they don't see any extra money to pay debt off. People are just getting by, paying the minimum payment due. We know it takes extra monthly money to pay on the principle of a loan to really get ahead. Most of the monthly scheduled payments in the typical loan are just on the interest. The majority knows this but assume that they need five part-time jobs to get that extra money.

Be of good courage! We have found that the average family has within its income the potential necessary to pay off their debts. I am going to take you through some loss areas that seem to plague the average family.

There are two things that every family MUST have in place to become debt free–and to stay debt free. The first is a sound budget, and the second is a cash reserve. A sound budget means that there is enough money to cover the existing living expenses. If your budget is not sound, take heart–there is still hope. This will be the first area to work on. Secondly, a cash reserve is usually non-existent in the typical family's budget. Without a cash reserve, you are open to suffering loss. Things do break and wear out in life, and without a cash reserve to pay these unexpected expenses, you are forced to use credit as your source of money.

Look at your budget sheet and see if the bottom line is negative or positive. Please be sure that your budget is a livable budget. Make it realistic! Although it is easy to write a budget, you must make sure that there is some room in it for gifts, pizzas, trips, etc. At this point, don't be so concerned about how well you plan your future budget but what your budget has been like for the last three months. You want to get a picture of where you are now. Only 15 percent of the families we see have an existing cash reserve. If you are a part of that percentage, then give yourself a pat on the back! If you are like most, then know that this is the second area you will need to work on. Most financial planners suggest a cash reserve of $5,000. Before you spend the time to build such a large reserve, we normally recommend a reserve of about $2,000 to start. This is enough to rebuild a car engine or buy a furnace. Relax. We will show you where the money will come from to put this reserve in place.

Now comes the fun part! We must find monthly cash flow with which to accelerate the debt. Before we start, be aware that we may suggest cutting areas of your life that you currently can't imagine living without. You must be convinced that freedom is worth more than material things. You've got to get to the point of being sick and tired of being sick tired over money. You may be required to change your lifestyle temporarily to achieve your plan, but the resulting freedom will be more than worth it!

Now, I want you to look for things in your home that are not being used. These items can be sold in a garage sale or consignment shop. We all have things in our lives that we think are so important, but reconsider them in light of your goal to be free. By selling unused items, we will begin our goal of putting that $2,000 cash reserve in place.

Next, look for things that have a monthly payment on them, such as a motorcycle or boat. Can you do without it? Maybe a used car could work just as well as the one with the $300 payment. Maybe the family could survive on one car for a while. These can be sold and the monthly payment can be put toward another debt. Some families own a home, and that in itself might be putting tremendous pressure on the family cash flow. It may be wise to sell the home and look for one that better fits your cash flow. Again, this may be a drastic measure for some, but you need to weigh these suggestions out. For most families, selling their home is unnecessary to accomplish their plan. I do not recommend selling such items as family heirlooms or antiques.

Be prepared for the I-feel-sorry-for-myself attitudes that may surface when you are faced with changing your lifestyle. When it comes to ridding your life of bondage, the devil always makes you feel like you are going backwards. Tell him to shut up.

After you are done with the above task, you will have some cash in your hand. If you have freed up some extra monthly income, then turn to the summary page at the end of this book and list the monthly freed-up cash there. Also make a note regarding how much you are still short of setting aside a $2,000 cash reserve. Remember, it is very important that you develop the cash reserve *before* you begin to pay off debt.

To Consolidate or Not To Consolidate?

The next step is to look at the existing debt, and determine if it could be restructured at a lower interest rate. The lower the rate, the faster it can be paid off because less money is required to pay on the interest.

The first loan to look at is the home mortgage. Depending on your current rate and the size of your loan, it may make sense to refinance. If you currently have a first and second mortgage on your home, you may want to consolidate them into one loan. Any lender can explain the benefits and details of any loan you are considering. Our company will also do this for you, free of charge. When you are contemplating refinancing consumer debt with mortgage debt, remember to factor in the tax benefits of the mortgage loan, which is deductible interest. A nine-percent second mortgage may be cheaper than an eight-percent consumer loan, considering your tax bracket. The old rule is that you should refinance your first mortgage if you can drop the interest rate at least one and a half to two points. This holds true for refinancing a first mortgage alone. If you are adding consumer debt to the new first mortgage, then you need to look at it a little differently. For example, if you have a current rate of eight percent on your first mortgage of $45,000 and you have $30,000 of high interest credit debt at 21 percent, you will save money by combining the debt in a new first mortgage at 8.5 percent. This would be a smart move, even though the new rate is slightly higher than the old first mortgage. Again, a lender can help you decide if it is in your best interest to refinance.

First mortgages can be used to pay off consumer debt if there is enough equity. Normally, a lender will allow you to go up to 100 percent loan to value when pulling cash out to pay consumer debt.

A second mortgage is normally used to consolidate consumer debt. The advantages are its tax-deductible interest (usually), and the fact that it normally has a lower interest rate than consumer debt. The danger in any consolidation loan is that you might start charging the credit cards back up afterward. We always advise cutting up the cards, even when no consolidation work is going to take place.

A traditional second mortgage or line of credit allows you to borrow up to 100 percent of the equity in your home. There are many lenders now that will allow you to borrow up to 125 percent of the equity. The same principle applies to determining the benefit of consolidating. Does it save you interest? Be sure to figure the tax advantages of the second when weighing this out.

Beware of the line of credit. Although a second mortgage may be placed as a line of credit, it usually has lower interest rates and closing costs than a fixed-end second mortgage. We recommend using only a fixed-end second mortgage. A fixed-end second mortgage means that there is a specific date when it will be paid off. A line of credit works just like a big credit card, and it may never be paid off if you keep pulling money from it. If you have had trouble with credit card debt, do not tempt yourself here. Check around for the best deal, cost, and rate.

If you do not own a home, you may consider consolidation with either a bank loan or in some cases a low rate credit card. Each issue of <u>Money Magazine</u> lists the lowest rate credit cards in the country. Again, be sure to CUT UP the old cards, especially after you have paid them off. Never apply for more credit than you are planning to consolidate if you are using credit cards to consolidate old debt. If your credit is such that you cannot qualify for a consolidation loan of any type, do not worry. You will still be able to develop a plan to be completely out of debt.

Another route to changing your present debt is to have a current lender either lower the interest rates or stop them all together. That's right! Most credit card lenders will change your rates and even stop all interest charges if a third party negotiates in writing on your behalf. There are many companies that do this type of work, such as Consumer Credit Counselors. However, you can do it yourself. Perhaps your church or someone you know that is in business can write the letter for you on his or her letterhead. If you are currently behind on your debt payments, then communication is the key. Don't wait to be called–you do the calling and keep your lenders aware of your situation. Remember, as Christians we want our word to be good regarding the debts we said we would pay back. Normally, bankruptcy should not be an option for Christians.

The Tax Refund Myth

Over two thirds of the U.S. population get a refund check from Uncle Sam every year and think it is the greatest thing since sliced bread, since they can't save money any other way. However, Uncle Sam pays zero percent on the money you overpaid during the year. Make changes now to leave about $200 in a refund check for next year, and put the increased cash flow on your summary sheet at the end of this book. Talk to your tax advisor or payroll department for detailed instructions on how to change your W-4. Be sure to include any new child, new home or new second mortgage when figuring your new allowance.

The Insurance Game

Every family has to pay for many different types of insurance. Our advice is to buy the least expensive quality insurance you can. To save money on insurance, set higher deductibles on deductible type insurance programs, such as auto, home and health. Setting higher deductibles will also require you to have a cash reserve in place to cover those deductibles in the event of a claim.

Be a good shopper when it comes to insurance. Rates vary between companies. You can obtain a list of every licensed company in your state by contacting your state insurance department. Some states even provide a comparison of prices for the companies in their state. Avoid specialty insurance policies like cancer or accidental death policies, which are very limited in their coverage.

Buy term life insurance. The life insurance industry makes its living by selling expensive cash value insurance, such as whole life, universal and variable life. You can buy the coverage for a lot less money by buying term. The cash values of an existing policy may provide your cash reserve or pay off some debt. If you want an analysis of your existing coverage, give us a call or talk to your insurance agent about term. Never terminate an existing policy before you have your new policy in your hands. Some medical conditions may prevent the issuing of a new policy, so it is always best to be sure before you change.

Group insurance may be your best route to obtain less expensive coverage. All group insurance has a limit, so check out the options with your employer. One thing to consider is that if you leave your company, you are usually leaving your insurance. Group insurance is a great way to boost your insurance program, but it should never be your complete insurance program. Always maintain personal life insurance outside of work. Check with your employer about options in raising or changing your coverage.

Cash in Low Yielding Assets

Many times, I find families that have low yielding investments, such as savings bonds or savings accounts, yet they have high-interest consumer debt. The mindset is, "I need to save for the future." By paying off consumer debt, you *are* investing in the future. If you pay a debt off that has a 21 percent interest rate, it is the same as investing that money at 21 percent with a guaranteed return. Fair or poor performing mutual funds, annuities, CD's, and stocks are other sources of cash.

Some retirement plans allow you to either take out or borrow the money, at either low interest rates or with no interest and no penalty. Check with your employer's benefit department before making any changes.

Regarding 401K's, we usually recommend that a family temporarily stop investing in their retirement accounts until they have paid off any consumer debt. Exceptions could be made if your employer has a high-matching rate over 50 percent, if you are in a high tax bracket, or if the contribution is mandated. A family that has debt with rates of 18 percent to 21 percent should focus all available cash towards these debts rather than retirement plans.

Things You Can Live Without

Most of the time, cable TV, special salon or nail care visits and health club memberships are not an essential part of life. Examine your current lifestyle. You might consider funneling some of that money toward your goals.

Reducing the Cost of Education

I often find families financially strapped with the cost of sending their children to private Christian schools. Sometimes homeschooling is an option that can free up cash. Besides, it is better for the children. Although most mothers cannot see themselves teaching their children, it really is easy because of all the material that is available. Most states contain statewide organizations to support homeschool families with curriculum and legal support. Homeschooled children regularly score higher in academics and advance faster in social and spiritual life. Ask your pastor if he knows of any families he could refer to you that home educate their children. He might be able to lead you in the right direction.

For children who are ready for college, post-secondary education may save you thousands of dollars. A child under the age of 18 can attend college free if their academics are fairly sound. This is paid for by the state. This benefit is even available for homeschooled children in many states. Contact your state's department of education for details.

Proper Tax Planning

If you are self-employed, it is very important to know how to take the maximum deductions when figuring your taxes. The IRS is a major enemy in your quest to be financially free. I know first-hand that when I restructured my business, I started saving thousands annually. You need to find good tax people who are more than processors, but who will go to bat to save you money. They should offer programs to educate you on software and tax strategies for running your business. There are many good publications on the market to help you save taxes. It is up to you to have knowledge. No one is going to watch over your money like you will.

According to Dan Pilla—who has written a dozen books on how to defend yourself against the IRS—the IRS must rebate penalties and interest on penalties. You can file for a rebate with form #843 once the tax has been paid. You only have two years to file for this rebate once the tax is paid. For more information on taxes you can purchase Mr. Pilla's books by calling 1-800-553-6458.

Money Magazine stated that 50 percent of those who challenge their property taxes save 10 percent. Contact your state auditor's office for details on how you can be sure you are not paying too much.

Most accountants agree that there is no better way to save taxes than to set up a family business. There are many books on the market that explain hundreds of home-based businesses which can be profitable, as well as save you a bundle in taxes. Pray about it, and then go for it.

The Reward

As you can see, there are many ways to free up money in the family budget. Sometimes, something as simple as a part-time job can make the difference needed to accelerate debt. The bottom line is that with a few changes, there is always money.

How did you do? You should have been keeping track of the money you were freeing up on the summary page. Now add up the summary page. This number represents the amount of freed monthly cash, which can now be used to accelerate debt. I have enclosed a copy of a sample debt acceleration plan at the end of this book. If you would like to have a complimentary plan made for your family, please contact Faith-Full Family Finances, Inc. You can reach our home office at 1.888.397.DEBT or 740.397.DEBT.

Put your trust in the Lord, and work hard. God promises to bless the work of your hands.

Monthly Cash Flow Savings

Item	Monthly Savings
1.	$
2.	$
3.	$
4.	$
5.	$
6.	$
7.	$
8.	$
9.	$
10.	$
11.	$
12.	$
13.	$
14.	$
15.	$
16.	$
17.	$
18.	$
Total Monthly Savings	$

Get Out Of Debt!

A Financial Plan to Freedom

for
YOU?

"The rich rule over the poor and the borrower is
servant to the lender." Proverbs 22:7 (NIV)

Faithful Family Finances
6040 Sharp Rd.
Mt. Vernon, Ohio 43050

1.888.397.DEBT

This work does not intend to take the place of advice from a tax attorney or represent legal advice. What follows is an illustration of a possibility. It was developed to share principles of money management. You may want to consult your CPA or tax attorney before actually following the plan.

PRESENT BUDGET FOR:
Jim and Kathy Ratliff

Net Income:

Jim $2,801.66
Kathy $1,640.00

Total Net Income **$4,441.66**

Tithes and Offerings $650.00

Expenses:
House/Rent $1,165.03

Consumer Debt:
Car Loan $365.00
Car Loan $301.02

Total Loan Payments $1,831.05

Credit Card Payments:
Visa $175.00
Discover $167.00
Sears $96.00
Home Depo $123.00

Total Credit Card Payments $561.00

Insurance Payments:
Auto..$55.00
Homeowners $31.00
Health $265.00
Life $102.00

Total Insurance Payments $453.00

Living Expenses:
Food $400.00
Telephone and Utilities $231.00
Auto, gas and expenses $110.00
Misc. newspaper, magazines, dues and gifts $30.00
Entertainment $50.00
Clothing $100.00

Total Living Expenses $1,021.00

TOTAL EXPENSES **$4,441.66**

SAVE BY REFINANCING YOUR HOME

OLD MORTGAGE

Current Rate	Payoff Balance	Monthly Payment
07.60 %	$155,000.00	$1,165.03

NEW MORTGAGE

Current Rate	Payoff Balance	Monthly Payment
05.60 %	$157,500.00	$904.17

TOTAL MONTHLY SAVINGS $260.86

Jim and Kathy Ratcliff

DEBT REDUCTION AND CONSOLIDATION

Debt Name	Interest Rate	Present Balance	Monthly Payment
---Unconsolidated Debt---			
Auto #1	7.00%	$18,400.00	$365.00
		Total: $18,400.00	$365.00
---Consolidated Debt---			
Debt Consolidated With New 2nd Mortgage			
Chase - Visa	22.00%	$5,600.00	$175.00
Sears	21.00%	$3,200.00	$96.00
Auto #2	9.00%	$3,540.00	$301.02
Home Depo	18.00%	$3,400.00	$123.00
Discover	19.00%	$7,300.00	$167.00
		Total: $23,040.00	$862.02
---New Debt---			
New 2nd Mortgage	6.00%	$23,500.80	$260.91
		Total: $23,500.80	$260.91

TOTAL MONTHLY SAVINGS $601.11

Jim and Kathy Ratcliff

MAXIMIZE YOUR I.R.S. DEDUCTIONS

Current Refund Check $2,000.00

Monthly Savings $150.00

Tax Savings From Consolidation $32.90

Does the IRS make free loans from you?

Can we really afford to be
making interest-free loans?

TOTAL MONTHLY SAVINGS $182.90

Jim and Kathy Ratcliff

ELIMINATE THE INSURANCE MIDDLEMAN

The following is a comparison based on several companies. You will need to check with your own agent to determine actual savings.

Automobile: Claims average every 4.7 years.

CURRENT DEDUCTIBLE	POSSIBLE DEDUCTIBLE	MONTHLY SAVINGS
$ 50.00	$ 500.00	$ 15.84

Homeowners: Claims average every 12 years.

$ 100.00	$ 1,000.00	$ 2.16

Health: Claims average every 7.2 years.

$ 100.00	$ 1,000.00	(savings included in Health comparison)

TOTAL MONTHLY SAVINGS .... **$ 18.00**

($216 saved a year)

1. Raise Deductible

2. **Auto and Home and price survey - FREE**

WARNING: Before changing deductibles, be sure you have the cash available to make up the increased out of pocket expenses if a claim is filed.

SAVE BY ELIMINATING EXPENSIVE
CASH VALUE INSURANCE

PRESENT PLAN

INSURED	COVERAGE
James	$ 150,000
Kathy	$ 100,000
Children	$ 5,000

Total Annual Premium..**$ 1,224**

PROPOSED PLAN

INSURED	COVERAGE
James	$ 335,000
Kathy	$ 165,000
Children	$ 10,000

Total Proposed Annual Premium...**$ 539.16**

Increase in Coverage..**$ 255,000**

TOTAL MONTHLY SAVINGS ....**$ 57.07**

ELIMINATE EXPENSIVE CREDIT LIFE INSURANCE

Credit life is costly because it is issued to everyone regardless of their health. Those of us that are healthy are the ones who are penalized.

TYPE OF LOAN	MONTHLY SAVINGS
Auto Loan	Paid Off
Auto Loan	Paid Off
Mortgage Loan	$ 55.00

TOTAL MONTHLY SAVINGS.. $ 55.00

SUMMARY

THE RESULTS OF ASSET MANAGEMENT
TOTAL MONTHLY SAVINGS

Refinance	$260.86
Consolidation	$601.11
Taxes (Withholding Changes/Second Mortgage)	$182.90
Cancel Credit Life Insurance	$55.00
Health Insurance Savings	$45.00
Free Checking	$8.00
Reduce Internet/Reduce cable	$10.00
Removed PMI on mortgage	$65.00
"Temporarily" stop 401(k)	$120.00
Auto and Home Insurance Survey	$18.00
Change Insurance Package	$57.07
Tax Planning	$100.00
Will / Pre-Paid Legal	($17.00)

CASH RESERVE

Cash reserve amount: $3,000.00
Save for 2.0 months to establish the cash reserve.
After the cash reserve is established, you begin accelerating the debt payoff.
Built entirely with monthly savings.

TOTAL MONTHLY SAVINGS $1,505.94

Jim and Kathy Ratcliff

NOW YOU ARE READY TO REAP THE BENEFITS OF ASSET MANAGEMENT

DEBT ELIMINATION
Begin by applying the $1,505.94 to reduce your
monthly debts starting with the highest interest rate loan.

Each time a loan is paid off, that payment amount is added
to the next loan to be accelerated.

First, the Cash Reserve:
Required reserve $3,000.00
The cash reserve will be established after 2 months.

Next, the Auto #1:
Original balance $18,400.00
Interest Rate 7.00%
Normal Payment $365.00
Balance at Acceleration $17,866.94
Accelerated Payment $1,870.94
The loan will be paid in month 12 after 10 accelerated payments.

Next, the New 2nd Mortgage:
Original balance $23,500.80
Interest Rate 6.00%
Normal Payment $260.91
Balance at Acceleration $21,332.72
Accelerated Payment $2,131.85
The loan will be paid in month 23 after 11 accelerated payments.

Total time required to build cash reserve and pay consumer debt is 23 months.

Continued on next page...

Jim and Kathy Ratcliff

MORTGAGE ACCELERATION PROGRAM

1. CURRENT LOAN
    A. Current Balance $157,500.00
    B. Annual Interest Rate 5.60%
    C. Scheduled Number of Payments Remaining 356
    D. Monthly Payment $904.17
    E. Balance at time of acceleration $151,671.00

2. ACCELERATION OF MORTGAGE
    A. Scheduled Monthly Payment $904.17
    B. Monthly Acceleration Amount $2,131.85
    C. Total Accelerated Monthly Payment $3,036.02
    D. Time Required to Retire Debt . . . . 56 Months
    E. Total time until you are DEBT FREE . . . . 6.8 Years (81 Months)

3. AMOUNT OF INTEREST SAVED
    A. Original Loan Payment Total $321,623.06
    B. Accelerated Loan Payment Total $197,439.05
    C. Total Interest Saved on Mortgage $124,184.01
    D. Total Interest Saved (All Debt) $135,417.90

Total Financial Freedom at Age
46

Jim and Kathy Ratcliff

INVESTMENT PROGRAM

Age at start of investment: 46

Amount of investment per month: $3,036.02

Year	Age	Amount at 9%	Months
4	50	$174,634	48
8	54	$424,606	96
12	58	$782,417	144
16	62	$1,294,590	192
19	65	$1,819,100	228

Year	Age	Amount at 5%	Months
4	50	$160,954	48
8	54	$357,463	96
12	58	$597,379	144
16	62	$890,292	192
19	65	$1,151,705	228

Current Investment Restructuring

Old IRA (mutual funds)	New Equity Indexed IRA (11% Bonus)
$21,000	$23,310

Old IRA (mutual funds)	New Equity Indexed IRA (11% Bonus)
1. Subject to market declines	1. Not subject to market declines
2. Principle not guaranteed	2. Principle guaranteed
3. Market performance	3. Market performance w/o the risk of loss
4. Possible broker or annual fees	4. No broker or annual fees

Jim and Kathy Ratcliff

CONCLUSION

Based on the preceding data, you could be free from all debt in 6.8 years.

The plan assumes that your budget is sound and that you have a cash reserve set up. (Please use the attached budget sheet for your records.) It also assumes that you are totally committed to being out of debt.

Based on your current income, you will avoid 2.9 years of slavery to lenders by following the plan. In a sense, it's like adding 2.9 years to your life. Think a minute about how good it will feel to be free from debt. You will be free to:

1. FOLLOW GOD'S DIRECTION FOR YOUR LIFE
Trust in the Lord with all your heart and lean not on your own understanding; in all your ways acknowledge him, and he will make your paths straight.

Proverbs 3:5 NIV

2. PROVIDE ADEQUATELY FOR YOUR FAMILY
If anyone does not provide for his relatives, and especially for his immediate family, he has denied the faith and is worse than an unbeliever.

1 Timothy 5:8 NIV

3. GIVE TO THE GOSPEL
"Bring the whole tithe into the storehouse, that there may be food in my house. "Test me in this, " says the Lord Almighty, "and see if I will not throw open the floodgates of heaven and pour out so much blessing that you will not have room enough for it."

Malachi 3:10 NIV

4. GIVE TO THOSE IN NEED
Remember this: Whoever sows sparingly will also reap sparingly, and whoever sows generously will also reap generously. Each man should give what he has decided in his heart to give, not reluctantly or under compulsion, for God loves a cheerful giver. And God is able, so that in all things at all times, having all that you need, you will abound in every good work.

2 Cor. 9:6-8 NIV

Faith Full Family Finances is committed to your plan to be debt free. Feel free to call us anytime you may need some advice. If you choose to use any of the companies that we have recommended we would like to thank you. That enables us to continue to help families without charge. We also teach church seminars and Bible studies. If your church or group would have an interest then give us a call.

Jim and Kathy Ratcliff